Charter Quay

The Spirit of Change

The Archaeology of Kingston's Riverside

Wessex Archaeology

Principal contributors

Phil Andrews, Jon Lowe, Karen Nichols,
Dr. Christopher Phillpotts, Andrew Powell

Published 2003 by The Trust for Wessex Archaeology Ltd
Portway House, Old Sarum Park, Salisbury SP4 6EB

British Library Cataloguing in Publication Data
A catalogue record for this book is available from the British Library

ISBN 1–874350–38–8

Designed by Karen Nichols

Printed by Henry Ling (Dorset Press) Ltd, Dorchester

Contents

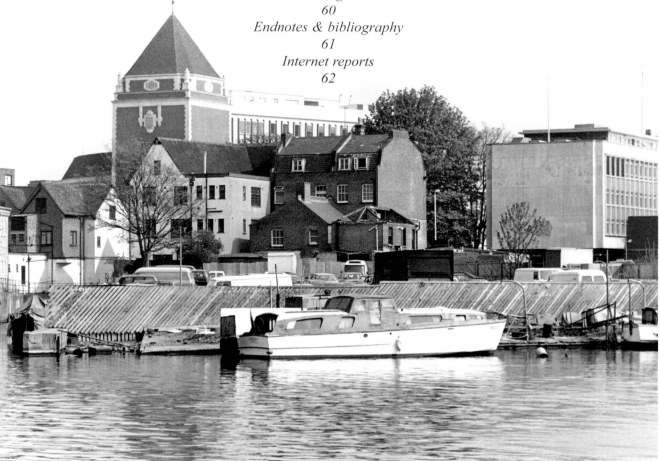

Forward by Duncan Hawkins
Archaeological Consultant, CgMs Consulting

This publication is the culmination of over fourteen years of documentary, stratigraphic, artefactual and environmental research on the Charter Quay site, Kingston upon Thames. Although the main period of work was undertaken in 1998–1999, the first archaeological intervention on the site actually took place in 1988. My own archaeological involvement at Charter Quay dates from 1990 when I project managed an archaeological excavation on the extreme south of the site.

In 1997 I was asked by the site developer, St. George, to organise a sustained programme of historic building recording and archaeological excavation, which was to be dovetailed into a comprehensive redevelopment programme. The success of this exercise is a credit to St. George, who provided the time, logistic support and crucial funding; to the Royal Borough of Kingston and English Heritage whose positive advice was of assistance at all stages; and to the dedicated team of documentary historians, building experts and archaeologists who carried out the work.

The investigation of the Charter Quay site has added significantly to our knowledge of the origins and development of Kingston upon Thames. Although it had long been known that Kingston originated as a late Saxon royal estate and administrative centre, there was little known about its development into a late medieval 'borough'. Now, we can say with some certainty that Kingston was deliberately 'planned' as a town in the second half of the 12th century, with a market place laid out south of a pre-existing settlement around All Saints Church, and bridges constructed over the River Thames and its tributary the Hogsmill, which had formerly made central Kingston an island.

Over the succeeding eight centuries settlement developed and intensified, with reclamation out into the Thames and Hogsmill, and encroachment around the fringes of the market place. The investigations have revealed much evidence of medieval and post-medieval Kingston's crafts and industries, providing clearer insights into the town's role as an inland port, articulating trade between London, Surrey and beyond.

During the course of the investigations significant public interest was shown in the progress of the work and the discoveries made. In response to this it was determined that the publication of the work should be made as accessible as possible, adopting a format that would appeal to a wide audience, while maintaining its academic integrity. This resulting volume will I hope reflect positively on the investigations and prove a relevant resource for all those who have an interest in the history and archaeology of early medieval England and the inter-relationship of the past and present.

Introduction

Charter Quay is not an ancient name like some of the street and place-names in Kingston upon Thames. It has been given recently to the large redevelopment site in the historic core of the town, lying between the River Thames, Market Place and High Street (*Fig. 1*). This area was part of a Saxon royal estate, and was at the centre of the medieval and later town, when Kingston was an important market and inland port. However, in the 19th and 20th centuries, as the focus of commercial activity shifted away from the Thames waterfront, the area became neglected, and has in recent years suffered a decline. Part of the town where once there were busy waterfronts, became characterised by derelict buildings, overgrown backyards and gardens, and temporary car parks.

The Charter Quay development once again makes the waterfront a focal point of town centre activity, linking the river with Market Place and High Street, and bringing a new vitality to the area. The excavations carried out during 1998–9, funded by St George in advance of their new development, have been the most extensive ever undertaken in the town (*Fig. 2*). With accompanying documentary research they have brought to light a continuous sequence of urban development, commercial growth and land reclamation that began in the early 12th century, and which in many ways reflects the wider history of Kingston upon Thames.

It was in the late Saxon period that settlement first became focused on an 'island' of gravel (bounded by the River Thames, the Hogsmill and other channels to the east and north) that was to become the centre of the planned medieval and later town. It is these processes of urban planning and development that the Charter Quay excavations have revealed. From the 12th century when the town's market place

Figure 1: The southern part of the site (Trench 2) under excavation in winter 1998. The River Thames with Kingston Bridge in the background, the High Street in the foreground, the River Hogsmill to the right and Emms Passage to the left.

and adjacent properties were first laid out, through the later medieval period when Kingston was an important inland port and market centre, and into the post-medieval and modern periods, with the advent of the modern department store.

A rare insight into the construction of the town's 12th century buildings, and the properties they once occupied, was provided by the discovery of several surviving house timbers from this period. Dismantled from a building on the market frontage they had been re-used in a riverside revetment (retaining wall) at the rear of the property, along a channel of the Hogsmill, where they had been preserved by waterlogging. The revetment itself represents the start of a long process of land reclamation extending back market frontage properties, aimed at protecting the town from flooding and facilitating river trade by the construction of wharves.

Although the Hogsmill, crossed by the stone Clattern Bridge, was regarded as the southern boundary of the town at this time, the excavations revealed the expansion of settlement and commerce to its south, along High Street, as shown by a timber building excavated on the corner of High Street and Emms Passage.

As the town grew in the later medieval and post-medieval periods, demand for land led to the subdivision of properties along Market Place and High Street, with new buildings extending backwards towards the river, some reached by alleys running between them from the street. There was also continued southward expansion, the area south of the Hogsmill acquiring an increasingly commercial and industrial character. This was reflected at the earlier Emms Passage property by a series of hearths, ovens and ancillary buildings, possibly for baking or malting, as well as by evidence of animal processing. Land reclamation also continued, eventually taking in a gravel bank at the mouth of the Hogsmill channel, as well as extending south along the bank of the River Thames. Some of the revetments were purpose-built, others incorporated re-used building and boat timbers.

An important feature of the post-medieval Market Place was the series of inns on its western side. Excavation on the site of the former Castle inn added many details to a documentary account of the inn's layout following its refurbishment in 1651. In addition, a dump of refuse deposited onto the riverbank at the rear of the Saracen's Head inn provided a fascinating glimpse of contemporary 'pub grub'. On the 'menu' were high quality cuts of meat – beef rib-steaks or crown-roast, veal, lamb chops and suckling pig – as well as fish, chicken and rabbit, plus mixed vegetables – cabbage, parsnip and possibly onion, leek or garlic – and fruits and nuts. Some of the remains may even represent a herbal hangover remedy.

The Castle, occupying Nos 5–6 Market Place, ceased trading in the early 19th century, and the property was divided into two shops. The shop at No 6 was eventually incorporated within Hide's department store (later Cardinal's), spanning Nos 6–9 Market Place. The recording of this large and frequently modified building, before its demolition as part of the site's redevelopment, revealed a number of historic features in its construction. These included 17th century and later cellars along its Market Place frontage, part of a contemporary range extending back from the street with elements of its tiled, hipped roof still preserved, and an elaborately carved staircase that had originally been part of the 1651 rebuild of the Castle inn. The layout of the building still retained evidence of the original medieval property boundaries.

The Charter Quay development represents a further important phase in the long, complex history of Kingston's waterfront and market place.

Background to the excavations

The redevelopment at Charter Quay has provided a rare opportunity to undertake large-scale excavations within the historic centre of Kingston and so study the development of the medieval and later town. The work, which began in 1998, funded by the site's developers, St. George, allowed the recording of the archaeological and historic remains immediately before construction began.

The development site (covering *c.* 1.65 hectares centred on Ordnance Survey grid reference TQ 1780 6915) lies between Market Place and High Street to the east and the River Thames to the west (*Fig. 3*). It is bisected by the Hogsmill river, which flows northwest through the site. The historical importance of the area has long been recognised, and the site falls within a zone of 'archaeological priority', as defined in the Royal Borough of Kingston's Unitary Development Plan.

Previous work

The programme of archaeological work undertaken by Wessex Archaeology in 1998–9 followed investigations in 1988–90 carried out by the Department of Greater London Archaeology (DGLA) in response to an earlier development proposal. Preliminary excavations to the north and south of the Hogsmill demonstrat-

Figure 2: A cross section through the site from the Market Place to the River Thames, showing the progressive stages in land reclamation.

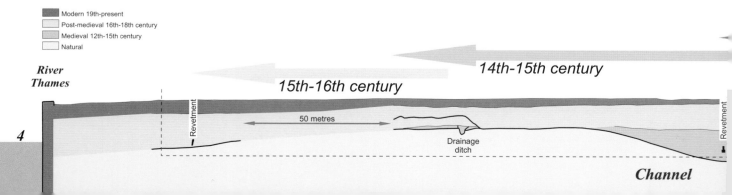

Modern 19th-present
Post-medieval 16th-18th century
Medieval 12th-15th century
Natural

River Thames

14th-15th century

15th-16th century

Revetment

50 metres

Drainage ditch

Revetment

Channel

4

Figure 3: The location of Charter Quay superimposed on the modern street plan (base image supplied by Cities Revealed ® aerial photography copyright The GeoInformation ® Group, 1999 Crown Copyright © All rights reserved).

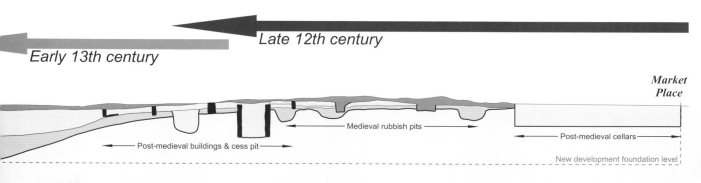

Late 12th century

Early 13th century

Market Place

Medieval rubbish pits

Post-medieval buildings & cess pit

Post-medieval cellars

New development foundation level

0   5 m

ed the survival of medieval deposits and waterfront revetments, while the excavation in 1990 of a large area (c. 550m^2) south of Emms Passage, revealed evidence for domestic, commercial and industrial activity, as well as phases of flooding and land reclamation, providing a cross-section of the land between High Street and the River Thames. Summary accounts of these investigations [1] were prepared, but there has been no overall report. As far as possible within this report, therefore, the results of the earlier work have been integrated with those from the 1998–9 excavation.

Excavation 1998–9

Before the 1998–9 excavation, an assessment [2] was made, based on all the information then available, of the nature, extent, importance and likely survival of the archaeological deposits within the site, and of the likely impact on them of the development proposals – which included reducing the ground level over a large area for basement car parking (*Fig. 4*). The assessment concluded that the shallow depth of soil sealing the deposits over much of the site ruled out the possibility of preserving them in situ. The Local Planning Authority asked, instead, that they be excavated and recorded, and English Heritage posed a series of research questions to be addressed by the excavation [3], relating to Kingston's development and changing economic role in the late Saxon (850–1066), medieval (1066–1500) and post-medieval (1500–1800) periods.

The first phase of excavation (October to December 1998) examined a large area off High Street, south of the Hogsmill (Trenches 1 and 2), with limited investigations off Market Place to the north (Trenches 31 and 32). Following the closure of Emms Passage, which crossed the High Street site, two further areas adjacent to Trenches 1 and 2 (Trenches 1A and 2A respectively), were investigated in

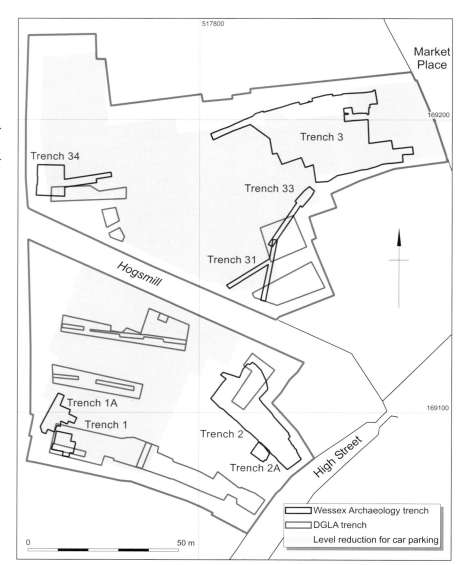

Figure 4: Plan of Charter Quay showing the excavated trenches and the areas of ground level reduction (archaeologically monitored) for underground car parking.

January 1999. The second phase of excavation (March to June 1999) was restricted to the Market Place site. Three small areas (Trenches 33, 34 and 35) were excavated during the main phase of demolition, following which a larger area (Trench 3) was investigated. Subsequently, the areas destined for basement car parking were archaeologically monitored while the ground level was lowered.

In addition, the historic fabric of the former Cardinal's department store on Market Place, which contained substantial post-medieval structural elements in its cellars, on its second floor and in its attic, was recorded before the building was demolished.

Documentary research provided a large amount of information about the site and its surrounding area, particularly about its likely topography and settlement history. The sequence of the site's development suggested by the research was largely borne out by the fieldwork, and helped inform both the excavation strategy and the on-site interpretation of what was found.

Before 1066
Prehistoric & Roman beginnings to Saxon royal estate centre

Geology and topography

The Charter Quay site lies on Pleistocene (Ice Age) deposits of river gravels (reworked Reading and Woolwich Beds) that form the flood plain terrace. In places, particularly in the lower lying areas, the gravels are overlain by 'brick-earth' and/or silts and clays probably laid down by the river.

The pattern and history of the various rivers and channels that flowed into the River Thames around Kingston are complex and not yet properly understood [4] (*Fig. 5*). However, recent archaeological work has indicated that the Hogsmill originally had an additional 'east arm', still active in the post-Roman period, that flowed northwards to the east of the town centre. This channel probably joined the 'Latchmere/Downhall channel', comprising the Latchmere stream (an existing watercourse) and the Downhall ditch (known from documentary evidence), before flowing west to the River Thames. These channels created a 'central island' on which the historic town of Kingston was sited [5]. The northern part of the Charter Quay site overlies the western edge of the island, the ground surface falling gently from east to west, and north to south – from *c.* 7.85m to 6.55m OD north of the Hogsmill, and from *c.* 6.90m to 6.40m OD to the south. The western half of the site would have been in the inter-tidal zone, comprising low-lying marginal land subject to regular flooding, and unsuitable for settlement.

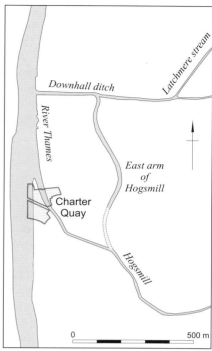

Figure 5: Map showing existing and former watercourses to the east of the River Thames around Kingston (after Hawkins 1996b) – only the Hogsmill survives as a channel today.

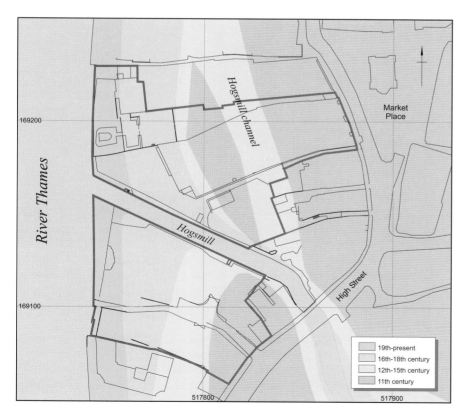

Figure 6: Kingston's changing riverline from the 11th century to the present, showing successive stages of reclamation.

7

The edge of the River Thames originally lay some 50m to the east of its present line (*Fig. 6*). In addition, a small gravel bank split the mouth of the Hogsmill into two channels (of which only the southern, now canalised, survives). The northern channel (unknown before the Charter Quay excavations) was *c.* 20m wide and ran north-north-west across the northern part of the site (*Fig. 7*), probably joining the River Thames south of the present-day Bishops Place House.

Prehistoric and Romano-British

Evidence of prehistoric and Romano-British activity has been found in and around Kingston. This includes a number of flint tools of late Upper Palaeolithic (30,000–10,000 BC) and Mesolithic (10,000–4,500 BC) date found in the town centre. The earliest evidence for settlement dates to the Neolithic (4,500–2,400 BC), the most important site being at Eden Walk (*c.* 150m east of Charter Quay), where Neolithic pottery, worked flint and animal bone were recovered from the channel of the former 'east arm' of the Hogsmill (*Fig. 9*). Neolithic axes have also been recovered from the River Thames, while a number of struck flints of probable Neolithic date were found at Charter Quay (*Fig. 8 & 10*).

Figure 7: Silts being removed down to natural gravel in the Hogsmill channel. The parallel lines of two 13th century timber revetments can be seen extending from the bottom right.

Figure 8: A typical Neolithic axe-this example is from the chalklands of Wessex.

The former river channel at Eden Walk also contained a brushwood platform or trackway of Middle Bronze Age date. Other Bronze Age (2,400–700 BC) features and finds were found during excavations at East Lane, South Lane and the Bittoms. These sites may represent part of a single, dispersed Late Bronze Age settlement to the south and east of Charter Quay. A now largely destroyed site at Kingston Hill may have been a Late Bronze Age defended settlement enclosed by a ditch, and the considerable quantity of metalwork recovered suggests that bronze-working may have been carried out there. A large assemblage of Bronze Age weaponry, some perhaps deliberately deposited as votive offerings, has also been retrieved from the River Thames.

Any traces of settlement along the River Thames and Hogsmill, however, are likely to have been removed by the scouring action of the rivers in flood, and this may be reflected in the small number of sherds of Late Bronze

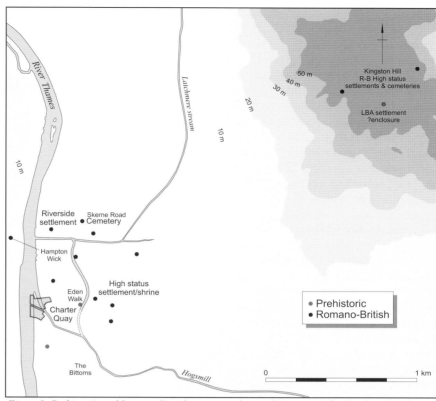

Figure 9: Prehistoric and Romano-British sites in and around Kingston (after Hawkins 1996b).

Figure 10: Flint knapping.

Age/Early Iron Age pottery that were found at Charter Quay. Although few Iron Age (700 BC–AD 43) finds have been recovered from Kingston, there was a Romano-British (AD 43–410) rural settlement and a cemetery *c.* 500m to the north of the site [6]. Recent work at Skerne Road has revealed Roman pits of 1st–2nd century AD date, with many broken box tiles, and the possible remains of a post-built building (Duncan Hawkins pers. comm.). Investigations in Hampton Wick, on the west bank of the River Thames, have also revealed evidence for settlement, and together these sites probably indicate the location of a fording point. A small quantity of Romano-British pottery was found at Charter Quay, supporting the picture of a generally low level of activity in the area, the riverside probably remaining as open ground used for grazing animals.

Saxon

There is evidence of early Saxon occupation on the higher ground east of Eden Street (**Fig. 11**). However, recent excavations at South Lane, *c.* 200m south of Charter Quay, indicate that there was also early to middle Saxon (AD 410–850) settlement on a gravel 'island' south of the Hogsmill. There is a late tradition in Kingston that the town had previously been called *Moreford* (marshy ford), a recollection perhaps of the earlier settlement [7], and that it had been re-founded in the late Saxon period, the focus of settlement shifting to the central Kingston 'island' during the 8th century. Charter Quay produced only two sherds of Saxon pottery probably due to the continuing low-lying nature of the site (**Fig. 11**).

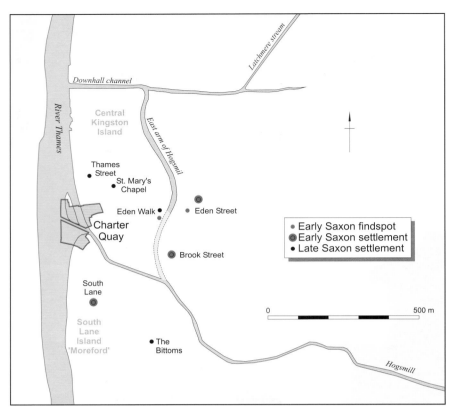

Figure 11: Saxon sites in and around Kingston (after Hawkins 1998).

Figure 12: Early Saxon pottery from Croydon. Sherds from Charter Quay would have come from similar vessels.

Documentary evidence suggests that in the 9th and 10th centuries, Kingston was not a village or a town but rather the administrative centre of a royal estate. The first reference to the name 'Kingston' (*Cyninges Tun* or *Cingestune* – King's tun, meaning royal manor) is in an agreement between Kings Ecgbert and Athelwulf, and Coelnoth, Archbishop of Canterbury, at a council held there on 20th November 838. This was a key moment in the establishment of the Wessex monarchy, and Kingston was clearly of sufficient prominence to be used as the venue for this important 'summit meeting'.

Because of its central location within a realm that comprised Wessex, Kent, Mercia and East Anglia, Kingston may have been a natural choice for such royal events although it was not itself a major focus of political power, and between 901 and 979 at least four (possibly as many as seven) Late Saxon (AD 850–1066) kings were crowned there (and a number of royal charters also witnessed there). Being near the tidal limit of the River Thames may have been significant for a dynasty that claimed to be kings of the sea. Moreover, its position beside the river placed it in what was probably regarded as a frontier zone between the power centres of the kings of Wessex and the archbishops of Canterbury.

The location of the royal estate centre, which is likely to have included a large timber hall, a church and ancillary buildings, is not known. It probably lay in the area now occupied by the parish church of All Saints and its churchyard (today somewhat smaller than in medieval times). This was the site of a chapel dedicated to St. Mary the Virgin – probably a late Saxon minster church in origin which is likely to have formed part of the royal complex (**Fig. 13**).

All Saints Chiurch – a 13th century building, but perhaps replacing or incorporating a substantial late 12th century church. The site of St Mary's lies in the foreground.

ually moved around their realms, and most of their retinue probably lived in tents. From the 9th century onwards, however, a small permanent settlement probably grew up around the royal complex, possibly to its north. Ditches of 9th–10th century date, perhaps dug both for drainage and as plot boundaries, have been found at Thames Street a short distance to the north of Charter Quay.

A late tradition says that two Saxon kings, Athelstan and Edwy, were crowned in the market place at Kingston, raising the question as to why no Saxon features were found on the market frontage at Charter Quay. Although the frontage had been almost completely destroyed by post-medieval cellars, it is likely that more Saxon material would have been present had there been occupation and a market place in that area. It may be that the 'market place' referred to was simply a large open area that only became formalised and built around as an act of town planning in the late 12th century.

The chapel, preserved as the traditional place of coronation of the first kings of England, survived until 1730 when it collapsed whilst graves were being dug inside. Although engravings of the building and excavations in the 1920s suggest that it was of 11th rather than 10th century date, it could have replaced an earlier timber church.

Despite Kingston's status, the settlement's extent may have been limited at this time – Anglo-Saxon kings contin-

Figure 13: Detail of an 18th century engraving of St Mary's Chapel. The doorway suggests an 11th century rather than 10th century date for the building.

Medieval urban expansion
Kingston flourishes 12th–13th century

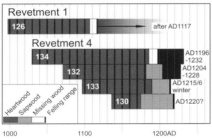

Figure 14: Bar diagram showing the dates of timbers from Charter Quay revetments 1 and 4.

The Town

By the time of the Domesday survey in 1086, Kingston had become the largest settlement in the Kingston 'Hundred', an administrative unit extending approximately from Kew in the north to Hook in the south, and from Malden in the east to East Molesey in the west. Within this, the extensive royal estate of Kingston had a population of more than a hundred families operating thirty ploughs on arable land, as well as meadow and woodland, fisheries and five mills. It is clear from the size of the estate that its central settlement, described as a *vill* held directly as part of the King's personal estate, had kept its earlier special status, although there was no evidence that it yet extended as far as the Charter Quay site and it may still have consisted only of a small village around the church and former estate centre.

During the 12th century, however, the village began to grow rapidly, and in 1200 was granted urban status by King John in a charter allowing the freemen of the town to pay him a fixed annual sum in return for becoming lords of the manor. Throughout the country there was rapid urban growth in the 12th and 13th centuries, mainly because of the great increase in trade, but an additional stimulus to the development of Kingston was probably the building, around 1170 [8], of a wooden bridge across the River Thames, the first bridge upstream from London. The stone Clattern Bridge across the Hogsmill, was built around the same time, as probably were two other bridges in the town (since vanished) over the east arm of the Hogsmill and the Downhall ditch – Stone Bridge and Barre Bridge respectively.

There is a documentary reference to a castle being captured at Kingston during the Barons' Wars in 1263–5, but this seems to have had little lasting effect on the town's progress. The town had no formal defences, such as a ditch and bank or circuit wall, although the surrounding watercourses, which effectively marked its boundaries, may have provided some protection.

Figure 15: 18th century view of Kingston showing wooden bridge over the Thames.

Around the market place

Although the area south of the church may have been used for buying and selling goods and produce from the late Saxon period, the excavations showed that the present market place was probably laid out as a deliberate act of town planning in the late 12th century. Other Surrey towns established in the same period, such as Reigate, also had market places at their centres.

Many of the Kingston's earliest buildings would have been on the market frontage, that section at Charter Quay being fully occupied by houses (possibly with street level shops and workshops) by 1200. The land behind, initially open to the River Thames, became progressively filled in with buildings such as workshops, stores and stables.

A charter for a market at Kingston was granted in 1208, and early documents list some of the traders that occupied properties on its western side, in the area of Charter Quay. Some had occupational surnames, such as *le Coliere* (charcoal supplier) and *le Orfevre* (silver/goldsmith). Few of the objects found there, however, appear to relate to these trades, although a sickle blade, several knife blades and an awl may have had more than simple domestic uses. Six whetstones, all in mica schist (a metamorphic rock probably imported from Scandinavia), would have been used for sharpening these and other tools.

Another market trader was *le Poter* (potter). Kingston was a centre of pottery production from the mid 13th century, documentary sources referring, for instance, to it supplying 3300 'pitchers' to the royal court between 1264 and 1266. Although pottery was by far the most common find at Charter Quay, there was no evidence of its manufacture within the site.

Figure 16: Examples of Kingston-ware pottery (copyright © of the Museum of London Specialist Services).

Medieval pottery production in and around Kingston

From the mid 13th century, Kingston was a major production centre of a type of pottery known as 'Surrey whiteware' [9], but it may also have had an 11th or 12th century pre-whiteware industry [10]. The earliest known Surrey whiteware kilns in Kingston were to the east of Charter Quay, around Eden Street and Union Street, but 'wasters' (spoilt vessels) from them were all of 14th century date. Nonetheless, the repertoire of Kingston's late 13th century potters can be seen in the range of Kingston-type wares excavated in London [11].

The discovery of a dump of whiteware wasters at Bankside in Southwark, in a fabric identical to the Kingston wasters, suggests that the Kingston industry may have been founded by potters from London. As the nearest source of iron-free white-firing clay was several kilometres away, the choice of Kingston for pottery production may be related to the ease of river transport for both raw clay and finished goods, the establishment of the town's market and its expansion of the town following the construction of the Kingston bridge.

The Kingston potters produced a range of highly decorated jugs, bearing vibrant polychrome motifs, stamped bosses and anthropomorphic forms, as well as plainer utilitarian forms. Most of the known range was found at Charter Quay. These included jugs, some of the late 13th century examples having applied (either stamped or rouletted) strips, pellets and pads within complex and highly decorative schemes. There were also coarsewares jars and bowls for general use, and more specialised cooking wares of mid-13th to mid-14th century date. Polychrome examples, coloured with copper and/or red slips, however, were rare, and none of the anthropomorphic forms was found, and there was only one curled horn from a zoomorphic vessel.

The popularity of Kingston wares in London declined in the later 14th century in the face of competition from the rival whiteware industries at Cheam (some 10km away) and those on the Surrey/Hampshire border. However, as a major market, the town probably remained a regional redistribution centre for the wider pottery industry – London-type wares, and 13th/14th century greywares from Hertfordshire, Berkshire and Surrey are all represented in the town [12]. At Charter Quay, however, they only occurred in small quantities, almost exclusively in jar and bowl forms (although a single jug handle was found), and the few sherds of imported pottery could all conceivably have come from a singe North French monochrome jug, decorated with applied scales (probably early 13th century).

Later medieval pottery was comparatively scarce at Charter Quay due, at least in part, to the increase in the use of vessels made of other material such as metal. The pottery includes Cheam, Coarse Border Ware, 'Tudor Green' and a small amount of late London-type ware, the assemblage being characterised by sparsely decorated jugs, bifid rim jars, and large bunghole jars or jugs. The Kingston pottery industry had one last flourish, although in a different guise – in 1979 a dump of late 15th/early 16th century redware wasters was found behind High Street, about 100m to the southwest of the Market Place. Vessel forms included jugs, bunghole pitchers, jars, cauldrons and pipkins, bowls and dishes, and costrels.

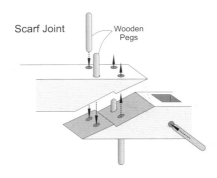

Scarf Joint   Wooden Pegs

Archaeological investigation of the market place frontage was hampered by the fact that later cellars had removed all traces of the earlier, timber buildings. This is not unusual, as little of any 12th century timber building survives from anywhere in the country. It is for this reason, that one of the discoveries at Charter Quay is of particular importance. It appears that a building on the market frontage had been dismantled, and several of its substantial oak timbers re-used in a riverside revetment at the rear of the property. Dendrochronological dating indicated that one timber had come from a tree cut down some time after 1117, but probably well before 1232, the latest possible date for the revetment's construction [13] (*Fig. 14*). The waterlogged conditions at the edge of the river ensured the timbers' survival, providing valuable help in seeing how some of the earliest timber buildings on the site were built. The pieces included part of a wall-plate – the horizontal beam running the length of the building at eaves level, and forming the top of its wall (*Fig. 17 & 18*). It would have been supported by vertical posts, and in turn born the weight of the roof. The building may have been dismantled when its posts had rotted and could not be easily replaced, or perhaps to coincide with a general phase of rebuilding in the town.

Figure 17: Detail of scarf joint used in the wall-plate.

Figure 18: The standing figures are marking the locations of mortise holes for the vertical posts that would have supported the wall-plate at eaves level.

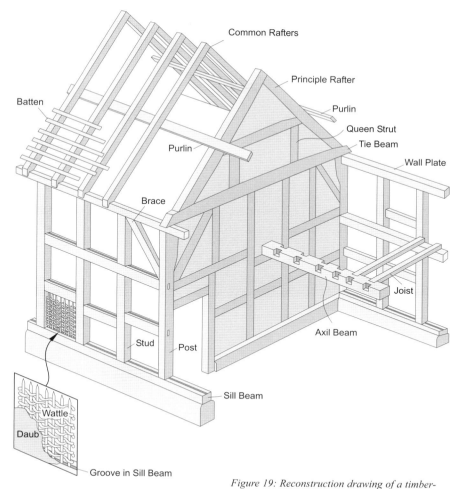

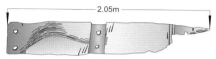

Figure 20: Part of a roof purlin reused as a post in revetment 1. The slots would have held rafters which were pegged in place.

Some of the many medieval nails found at Charter Quay may have come from such buildings, although timbers were usually joined with wooden pegs (as in the wall-plate). Of particular interest, however, was a large box pad-lock, probably fitted to a door. Other structural items included five clench bolts, two hinges, one hinge pivot, a looped spike and a looped staple.

Figure 19: Reconstruction drawing of a timber-framed building showing structural elements.

Figure 21: Box Padlock.

Evidence of a timber building' construction

Part of a wall-plate, comprising two joined timbers, from a dismantled timber building of probable late 12th century date, survived to a length of 7.5m in a riverside revetment west of Market Place. The longer timber, which was complete, measured 4m, while the other had been cut rather crudely with an adze, perhaps to make it easier to move. The timbers (made of the boxed-heart of a tree's trunk) had been roughly shaped to a rectangular cross-section measuring c. 0.25m by 0.15m, then neatly joined using a scarf joint (Fig. 17) held in place by four oak pegs or treenails. The joint (a through-splayed and tabled scarf, here with the joint surface of the underlying timber slightly recessed) is a type known in buildings dating from c. 1190 until the later 13th century. Part of a wall-plate with a simpler form of scarf joint has recently been found in the City of London dated to the 11th century [14].

Each section of the wall-plate had a number of mortise holes cut through it, set about 1.5m apart (Fig. 18) (although there were two adjacent mortise holes at the northern end). The mortise holes would have held the tenons on the ends of the vertical posts on which the wall-plate rested, with pegs driven through to secure them in place. The vertical posts would either have been set earth-fast in post-holes, or would have rested on horizontal timber sills, sill-mounted timber-framed structures being introduced between 1150 and 1250 [15] (Fig. 19).

Because the upwards facing surface of the scarf joint lies next to one of these mortise holes, it is clear that the wall-plate was found the right way up – had the wall-plate originally been the other way up, downward pressure from the eaves would have caused the joint to sep-arate. As it is unlikely that this type of joint would have been used in a sill-beam, at the base of the wall, it is clear that the other timbers fixed to the wall-plate in the revetment – slotted posts holding in place horizontal planks – were placed there during the revetment's con-struction, and did not form part of the building's structure.

One other large building timber had been used to extend the revetment northwards. It was at least 2.05m long, 0.26m wide and 0.13m thick, one sawn end surviving intact, the other broken. On one side were the remains of three half-lap joints (Fig. 20), 0.15m wide and 0.75m apart, each with two peg holes, two of the joints having both pegs still in place. It may have been part of a side purlin, a horizontal roof timber giving support to the rafters. These have not been recorded in buildings before the mid-13th century, although this may reflect the rarity of surviving buildings of this date. The roof was probably covered with thatch, although cleft oak clapboard, shingles, or even turf could have been used.

Over Clattering Bridge

The stone 'Clattering Bridge' across the Hogsmill, named after the sound that horses' hooves made as they crossed it, also dates to the late 12th century, original elements surviving in the now widened Clattern Bridge (*Fig. 22*). The river marked the formal southern boundary of the town, it being recorded, for instance, that in 1253 the tenants of Merton Priory's manor of Canbury refused to perform watch duties south of the 'creek' at the end of the market as this was outside the town limits. Nonetheless, the land west of High Street, between the Hogsmill and Emms Passage, known in the 1290s as *Clateringbrugende*, had developed in the 12th century as a small suburb of houses and yards. The pattern of property boundaries suggests that there had been piecemeal settlement, advancing from the Clattern Bridge in a series of small-scale reclamations of the shores of the River Thames and Hogsmill. The road-way south of the bridge was called *Westbitamestrete* in 1314 (later West-by-Thames Street, now High Street).

Figure 22: The Clattern Bridge over the Hogsmill. Although the bridge has been rebuilt parts of the pier bases date to the late 12th century.

Evidence for early activity in *Clateringbrugende* was found to the south of Emms Passage in 1989, in the form of rubbish pits, post-holes and stake-holes thought to pre-date 1200. In 1998, the Charter Quay excavation north of Emms Passage found the post-holes of a timber building fronting onto High Street, dated to the late 12th or early 13th century (*Fig. 23*), and so about a century later than the earliest evidence for buildings on the market place.

Figure 23: Archaeologists at work on the complex sequence of medieval deposits on the High Street frontage in Trench 2 - these included post-holes, floor surfaces, hearths and ashy layers.

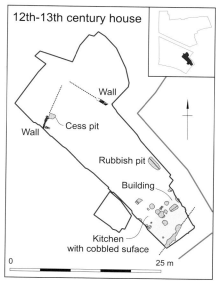

Wall

Cess pit

Wall

Rubbish pit

Building

Kitchen
with cobbled suface

0   25 m

Figure 24: The somewhat irregular pattern of gully and post-holes reflects the ground plan of a building of which no other traces survive.

The riverside property on the south side of the mouth of the Hogsmill is first known to have been occupied by Symon le Merchaunt, his name indicating his occupation. In 1298, his son Ralph divided the yard and its grange (presumably a barn used as a warehouse) into eastern and western parts, selling off the latter with access for carts and animals. Other trades south of the Hogsmill included butchers and a chandler. The only coin of this period recovered from the site was a silver penny of Henry III (1216–1272). It is unlikely to have been in circulation much beyond 1279 – the date of a major reform of the coinage.

Widening the Hogsmill in the 1950s.

A High Street property

Two insubstantial rubble walls, some 30–35m back from the High Street frontage, were probably built in the 13th century and may, therefore, mark some of the earliest property boundaries in the area. They defined parts of the northern and western sides of the property of a timber building on Westbitamestrete.

All that survived of the building itself was an arrangement of post-holes and a slot (*Fig. 24*). These indicate that it had been at least 8m long and *c.* 4m wide, fronting onto, and aligned parallel with, the street. At the front it appears to have had either a sill beam, or posts, set within a trench, while at the rear there were posts set within individual post-holes, possibly representing a transitional form of building between those with all earth-fast posts and those with timber-framing.

Behind the building, a hearth, several stone post-pads and the remains of a cobbled floor indicate the presence of a small structure, possibly a kitchen - it was common in the early medieval period to have a separate kitchen to reduce the potentially disastrous effect of a hearth fire. Some of the pottery found at Charter Quay (most of it Kingston-type wares), such as the jugs, jars and bowls, as well as more specialised cooking wares such as pipkins, frying pans and dripping dishes, throws light on these kitchen and other domestic contexts.

There was little evidence for other structures at the rear of the property, the area, perhaps subject to flooding, probably remaining as an enclosed yard. Slight traces of wall footings survived in the south-west corner of the yard, and there was a nearby square pit - possibly a cess pit. A larger, irregularly shaped, rubbish pit was dug closer to the building. The boundary walls to the rear had been built across a shallow depression which had been filled, partly deliberately, with gravel and other materials during the 13th century. This may mark the beginning of land reclamation in the area.

Topography, properties boundaries and land reclamation

The presence of the former channel of the Hogsmill affected the topography of the medieval town west of the market place. It marked the western edge of the 'island' on which the central core of Kingston was built, so influencing the layout of streets and alleys, the shape of the market place, and the boundaries of adjoining properties to the west. Although there was a gradual reclamation of land throughout the medieval period, the channel broadly defined the limit of building in this direction until the 17th century *(Fig. 25)*.

The 12th–13th century buildings, which would have included shops and workshops as well as domestic accommodation, were set within what were originally relatively large plots of land – wide enough to allow the buildings to be built parallel with the street. Such plots were often laid out to standard widths, using the 'perch' or 'pole', a unit of length varying locally between *c.* 3m and 7.3m. The three original plots on the market frontage appear to have been *c.* 10–12m wide, while that on the High Street frontage may have been just under 10m. Most property boundaries are likely to have been marked by wooden fences, although those off High Street appear to have been marked by rubble walls.

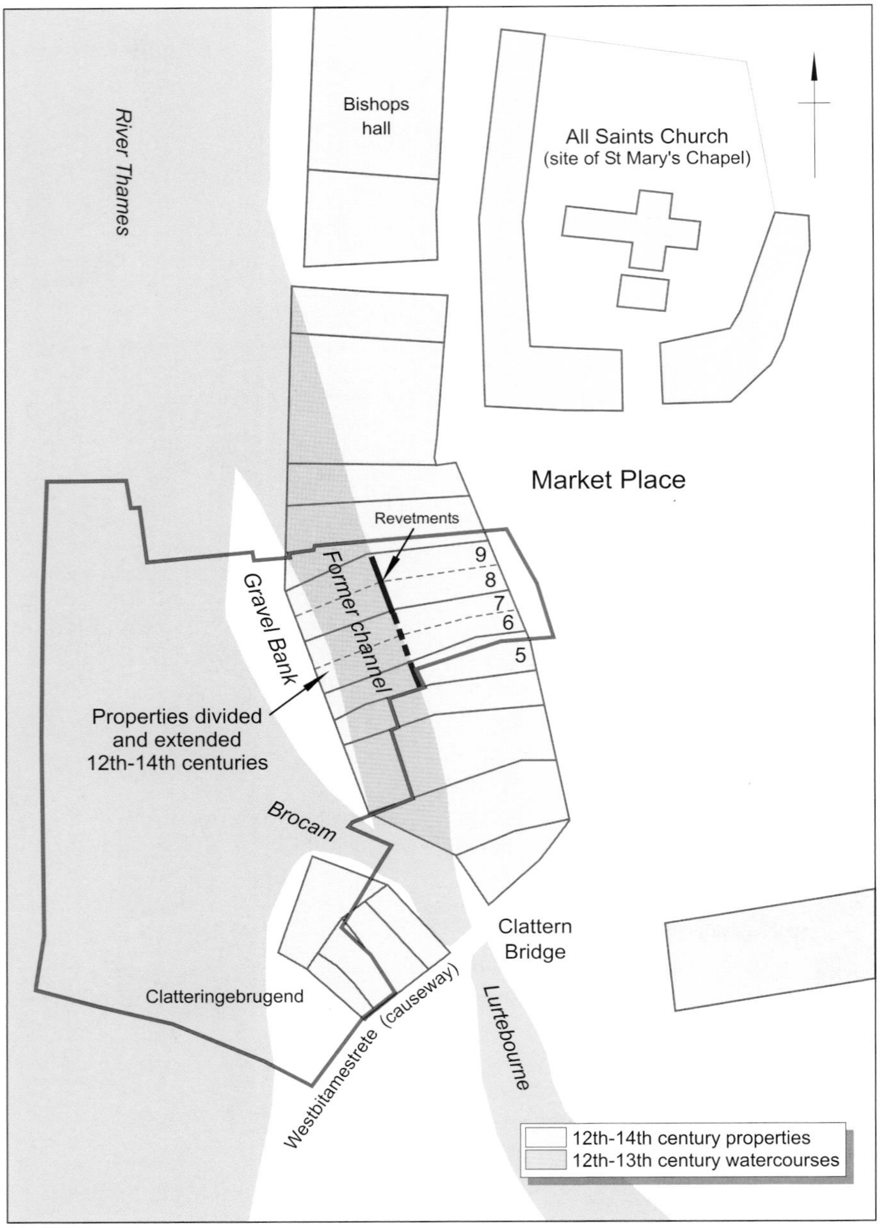

Figure 25: Topography and schematic layout of properties around Charter Quay in the 12th and 13th centuries.

Land reclamation at the Hogsmill channel

The earliest revetment (Revetment 1) comprised a re-used wall-plate that may have been moved some 50m from the market frontage to the edge of the channel, as well as other timbers possibly derived from the same building. As the two parts of the wall-plate were still joined, with the pegs of the joint still in place, it is clear that it had been moved as a single piece. The wall-plate formed the revetment's base plate.

The existing mortise holes in the base plate may have been enlarged, as they were now used to hold the full width of revetment's vertical timbers – four still held vertical posts pegged to it *(Fig. 27)*. The post in the hole at the southern end of the wall-plate, and that in the outer of the two adjacent holes at the northern end, had been driven into the ground to hold the wall-plate in place. The vertical posts, which measured *c.* 0.2m by 0.15m in cross-section, survived to a height of *c.* 0.5m, representing the level of waterlogging, but it is not clear to what height they originally stood - it is unlikely to have been more than 1m. The posts had slots cut into one or both sides to hold horizontal oak planks, three of which survived along the base. The planks were *c.* 1.50m long, 0.25m wide and up to 0.07m thick, with chamfered the ends to fit the slots. This method of construction (termed 'bulwark construction') is well known from revetments London in the early medieval period [16] *(Fig. 28)*. 'Blind' mortise holes (not going right through the timber) had been cut towards the outer edge of the wall-plate, midway between the main posts, and may have held smaller vertical timbers providing further support for the planks.

Properties further back from High Street may have extended as far as the River Thames, while those on the market reached back to the edge of the former Hogsmill channel. Within the latter properties, in particular, were a number of large pits that appear to have been dug for rubbish disposal. The gravel from them may have been used to create yard surfaces or paths around the buildings.

A series of riverside revetments at the Hogsmill channel illustrates the land reclamation process (*Fig. 26*). The earliest (Revetment 1), incorporating the re-used wall-plate, was built in the early 13th century. It was almost 10m long, probably representing the width of the property, showing that land reclamation was undertaken within individual plots, rather than collectively by groups of property owners. Although building timbers have been found in later revetments (generally of 14th century date) elsewhere along the River Thames in Kingston [17], these have invariably been made of smaller pieces, such as vertical studs (which formed the infill of the timber-framing) being re-used as posts. The timbers in Revetment 1, therefore, are not only earlier than those previously discovered, but are also more substantial.

Figure 26: . The two early 13th century timber revetments (R1 to the right and R4 to the left) along the east side of the channel being cleaned prior to recording.

Three later revetments were recorded, each *c.* 1m further into the channel on the same property. The inner two (Revetments 2 and 3) were made of wattle, of which only a few of the stakes and some fragments of the horizontal hazel rods survived (*Fig. 29*).

The westernmost revetment (Revetment 4) had a different method of construction again. The surviving section consisted of two lengths of a sub-square base plate (each *c.* 0.12m square and 2.5m long) laid end to end, supporting at least two layers of horizontal planking (*c.* 0.18m by 0.04m and 2.5m long), one on top of the other. The whole structure was held in place at the front by vertical posts (up to 0.25m square) driven into the underlying gravel, with redeposited gravel, silt and other debris being dumped behind it. Rather than being made of re-used building timbers, however, most of the revetment appear to have been specially made. This seems to be confirmed by the dendrochronological dates from the structure. One post, which still had its bark being, was dated precisely to the winter of 1215/6, while other timbers (a base plate timber, a plank and two further posts) indicated felling dates of between 1196 and 1232, all the dates being consistent with the early 13th century pottery recovered from the associated deposits (*Fig. 14*).

Figure 27: Detail of the wall-plate showing posts, mortise holes and surviving part of wall planking.

Figure 29: Recent stabilisation of riverbank at Wilton (Wiltshire) using wattle – similar to that found between revetments 1 and 4.

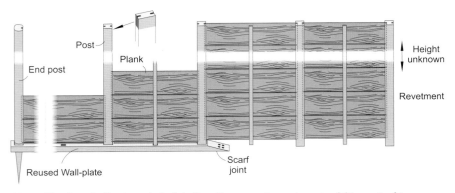

Post

End post

Plank

Height unknown

Revetment

Reused Wall-plate

Scarf joint

Figure 28: . Detail of horizontal plank-built wall construction – elements of this survived in Revetment 1 at Charter Quay.

The revetment would have had a dual purpose. Firstly it extended westwards the market frontage property (***Fig. 30***). Three later revetments on the same plot (Revetments 2–4) each encroached further into the river channel, and it may have been this process that is referred to in an early 13th century document. This records that, *c.* 1220, some land was reclaimed from the River Thames by the townsmen, for which *purpresture* (the wrongful encroachment on other's or common land) the royal Exchequer attempted to charge them rent. However, they contested the charge on the grounds that the River Thames had washed the land away again.

Their predicament hints at another possible reason for the revetment – to raise the height of the riverbank and so reduce the danger of flooding. The threat of flooding is likely to have increased after the bridge at Kingston was built, as it would have slowed the flow of the River Thames upstream causing an increase in silting, particularly around the mouth of the Hogsmill. Flooding is recorded at regular intervals in Kingston during the second half of the 13th century – in the 1250s, 1260s and 1280s.

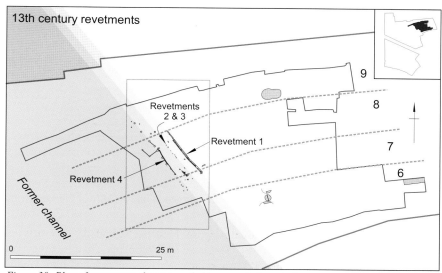

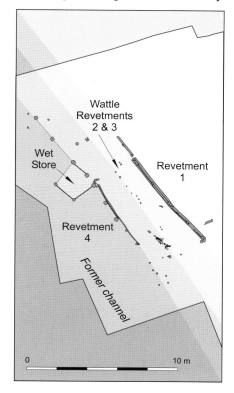

Figure 30: Plan of revetments showing probable property boundaries.

there was a fishmonger on the west side of the market place, and there are documentary references to salmon fisheries on the River Thames at Kingston (*Fig. 36*).

Most of the charred plant remains represent domestic waste, such as from food preparation, medicinal use, strewing herbs or additions to fuel. The charred seeds are probably the remains of baking, brewing and other culinary

Figure 31: Detail of revetments 1-4.

Diet

The animal bones and plant remains recovered from refuse pits (*Fig. 32*) and hearths throw light on the diet of the 12th and 13th century inhabitants of Charter Quay, as well as on some of the industrial and commercial activities undertaken there.

Of the small amounts of animal bone recovered (mostly from pits), most was butchery and meal waste, rather than primary slaughter waste. The majority were from domesticated animals, in particular cattle and sheep, the only evidence for hunting being one bone of an immature fallow deer. The sheep remains include some skull fragments that had been split in half to remove the brain. Pig bones were also present, and one pit contained part of the right foreleg of a horse (plus a number of frogs that had fallen in). The bird bones were mostly from domestic fowl and geese, although a pair of wing bones, both with their wing tips cut off, could be from the white-fronted goose, a winter visitor.

Fish bones included several from good-sized plaice, and a ling vertebra, both of them sea fish, probably brought in via London. No freshwater fish were recorded, which is surprising given the discovery in the Hogsmill channel of possible 'wet stores' where locally caught fish, in particular salmon and eels, could have kept alive or fresh before being sold. It is known

The 'wet stores'

A curious structure built into the front of Revetment 4, and contemporary with it, may have been used as a 'wet store' (*Fig. 33*). It was *c.* 2m square, projecting out into the river channel, with substantial posts at the corners and one course of planking surviving on all but the north side. The planks had been mortised into the posts, but were not re-used building timbers and had been made as part of the structure. The planking on the south and west sides would have prevented silting while allowing a flow of water through the structure, and the north side may have been closed by a wattle panel which could be moved to allow access and cleaning.

A larger wattle-lined container of probable 14th century date was recorded during earlier excavations around Kingston Bridge, and within this were found several 'knees' – wooden brackets holding together the frame of a boat – which were being stored wet prior to use. However, the small size of the 'wet store' structure built into Revetment 4 makes this interpretation less likely, as does its location within a shallow channel upstream of Kingston Bridge.

A re-used bucket (or barrel) found further out into the channel in the same property also appears to have been used as a 'wet store' (Fig. 34). The bucket, with its bottom removed, was supported on two short lengths of elm laid flat in the bottom of the channel. These were trimmed flat on their upper sides, with a further, thinner, and more irregular piece used to tilt the bucket slightly forward. The upper part of the bucket did not survive and it is not clear how it was held in place, but it was clearly set up in a way that allowed water to circulate within it and so keep its contents fresh. The bucket itself was of quite sophisticated construction, built of staves bound together round the outside with split hazel withies, themselves wound round with even thinner strips of hazel (Fig. 35). This binding appears to have covered the entire outside of the bucket.

Figure 32: . A section being drawn through a late 12th /13th century rubbish pit.

Figure 34: Reused stave-built barrel with its bottom removed in bed of channel. Was this, like the 'wet container', used for keeping salmon, eels or oysters wet – or did it serve some other purpose?

Figure 33: Revetments 1 and 4 looking southwest. Note the square 'wet container' between the two archaeologists on the right.

uses, as well as of animal fodder, while non-arable weeds, such as heather, bracken and sedges may indicate the use of plants for bedding, flooring, thatch or animal litter. The preliminary processing of the cereals, involving the separation of the grain from the chaff and the removal of weed seeds, would have been carried out in the country-side following their harvest, the grain brought to the town requiring only a final 'cleaning'. The accompanying weed seeds show that they came from both sandy and chalky soils. Fragments of two quernstones (import-ed from Germany), made from vol-canic lava, provide evidence for the grinding of cereals, and there were parts of two Purbeck marble mortars that would also have been used in food preparation.

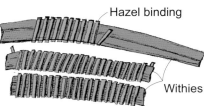

Hazel binding

Withies

Figure 35: Detail of the hazel withies following removal of the staves. The withies themselves were individually bound with thin strips of hazel.

Figure 36: Reconstruction drawing of wattle-lined fish ponds at Reading Abbey.

Cereals remains in pits

One pit contained a quantity of barley grains, with only very small amounts of other cereals and weeds being present, suggesting a single crop. Most of the plant samples, however, contained a variety of cereals, one pit, for example, producing a mixture of wheat, barley, oats and rye, and possibly also peas. The absence of chaff or weed seeds in the mix suggests it was debris from a store of cleaned grain.

In contrast, a hearth that produced mainly oats also contained a large amount of oat chaff, as well as plants of grassland, heathland and woodland. Given the presence of chaff, suggesting that the crop had not been threshed, the oats may have been fodder for horses, the grassland plants, including grasses, buttercups, vetches and tares, representing hay.

The Town

Kingston prospered during the 14th and 15th centuries and the town continued to grow. At Charter Quay many properties were divided into narrower plots although these were extended westwards as more land was reclaimed, and new timber buildings, on stone and tile foundations, were erected over a much larger area than before. Timber revetments began to be built on the River Thames waterfront, providing defence against flooding, protecting the riverbank from erosion and creating simple quaysides ('wharfage') for boats to load and unload.

There was a change in use of the Charter Quay area, possibly resulting from a change in ownership, with increasing 'industrial' activity. The London Charterhouse, a religious house founded in 1370, acquired the considerable Kingston property of John Wenge as part of its initial endowment, and the priory continued to purchase property in the town during the 15th century. The estate came to include a large part of the Charter Quay site west of Market Place, all land between the Hogsmill and Emms Passage, and some of that to the south of Emms Passage, as well as land further up the *Lurtebourne* (Hogsmill). The estate's houses, fields and meadows were normally leased individually to tenants.

Behind le Hyerowe

The Borough Charter of 1441 established the market's rights, and documents of the period list those occupying properties on its west side – a baker, fishmonger, vintner, sawyer, skinners, brewer and a hosier, as well as a number of inn-keepers and some

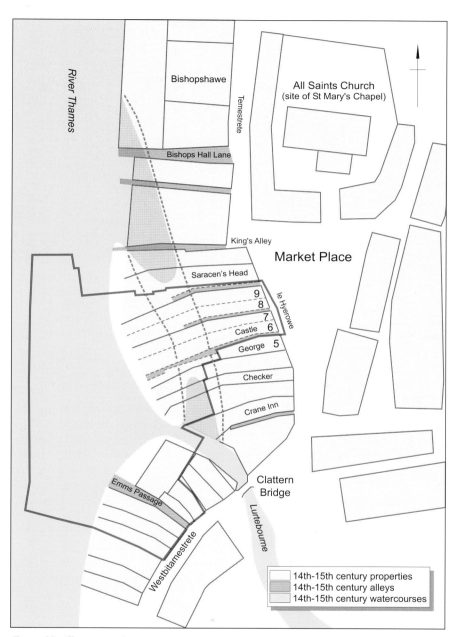

Figure 37: Alleyways such as Emms Passage provided access between the Market Place and High Street and the waterfronts alongside the River Thames and Hogsmill.

properties paid for the right to have stalls in the street and the market. Wool, leather and cheese are known to have been sold there, and the few coins found, which included a relatively unworn groat of Edward III (1327–1377) (worth about 4d/2p) and two worn silver pennies of late 14th or early 15th century date, reflect the commerce of the area.

Figure 38: Excavating the foundations of a series of medieval buildings constructed over the edge of the infilled channel.

The inns included the *Saracen's Head* at the north of the site, dating to at least a generation before 1417 (***Fig. 37***). To the south, the *George* was part of the Charterhouse estate and was leased out by it in 1442, 1455, 1474, 1483 and 1492–3. Further south again was the *Checker* which, like the *George*, was also probably established in the 15th century. Although, of the market place businesses, only the inns have been identified, one property with a sequence of large hearths may have been the bakery, and some of the buildings abutted a lane leading towards the river called *Souteresrowe* ('shoemakers' row'), where it was customary to sell shoes. Leather found preserved in dumped, waterlogged deposits behind several of the late medieval revetments included fragments of shoes (including complete soles) and offcuts, possibly the waste from shoe manufacture and repair.

Medieval towns lacked the luxury of space enjoyed by rural communities, and long narrow properties ('burgage plots') were laid out to maximise the number of traders in the market place. These usually combined a shop or store and a dwelling along the street frontage, in some cases with workshops or other buildings. However, the rentals of 1383, 1417 and 1427 indicate that, as pressure on land increased, a number of properties on the west side of the market were divided lengthways. This led to narrower properties, usually the width of a single bay of a timber-framed house, up to 5m wide, as was the case at Charter Quay. The new buildings were built at right-angles to the street, with the gable end of the roof at the front, and the main entrance opening onto an alley or passage at one side. As a result, any enlargement of the buildings would have been either vertically, by adding another storey, or to the rear, resulting in long, narrow buildings. The interiors of such buildings would have enjoyed minimal daylight. The terrace of buildings running south to Clattern Bridge was known as *le Hyerowe*, presumably because of the height of its buildings.

There was also some encroachment onto the market place, as reflected in the rental of 1417 which records several sets of posts in the street, probably to support jettied upper stories extending over the ground floor. Sets of posts were certainly present outside the *George* and the *Saracen's Head* inns. In 1427, for instance, the tenement of Edward Lusthill (which is probably identified with the *Saracen's Head*) was extended six and a half feet (1.98m) into the market place over its entire width of 13ft (4m) in order to build a new frontage.

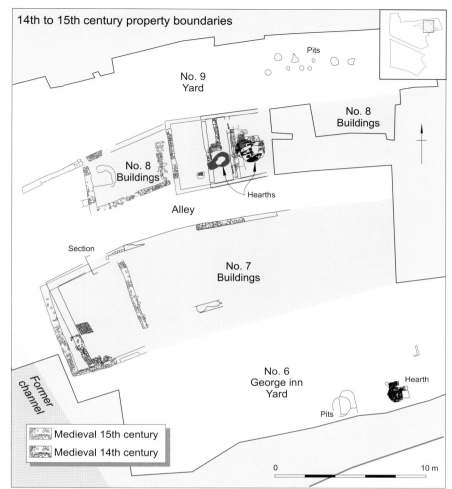

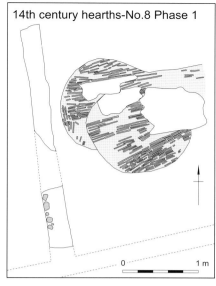

Figure 40: Plan of 14th century hearth.

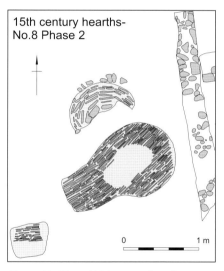

Figure 41: Plan of 15th century hearth.

Figure 39: 14th to 15th century buildings at Nos 7 and 8 Market Place.

The earliest surviving traces of cellar on the market frontage belong to the 16th–17th century, but there may have been earlier, medieval cellars or undercrofts, similar to that excavated in 1986, and now displayed, beneath the John Lewis store, north of Kingston Bridge. Most of the wall footings of the late 14th and 15th century timber-framed buildings were built of a characteristic mix of Reigate stone and flint, with regular levelling courses of roof tiles, all set in mortar. Despite the availability of roof tiles it seems that

No 8 Market Place

Excavation at No 8 Market Place revealed at least three phases of late medieval building (*Fig. 39*).The earliest building (phase 1), which stopped 5m short of the former edge of the Hogsmill channel, was *c.* 4.5m wide, although post-medieval rebuilding had destroyed both north and south walls. Towards its western end, a partition wall created what may have been a small storeroom with a further division in its northwest corner. East of the partition wall was a sequence of at least two large, keyhole-shaped hearths (*Fig. 40*). Each had a circular clay-domed chamber to the west and a long flue to the east, their floors being made of closely-packed, broken roof tiles set on edge.

After some 20–30 years the building was demolished and rebuilt, extending further to the west (phase 2). The earlier walls were largely robbed out, or taken down to ground level. The new building's western wall and a (rebuilt) internal partition wall each had a large 'slot' in the top, presumably to hold the vertical posts of the timber-framing. An internal east-west wall, overlying the two earlier hearths, abutted the partition wall, while there was a sequence of two new hearths in the room to the west, similar to the earlier ones, but with their flues facing west. A third, much smaller, square hearth in the same room would have had a different use (*Fig. 41*).

Subsequently, the partition wall was widened, the east-west internal wall dismantled and two new pitched-tile hearths built (phase 3) (*Fig. 43*). These were smaller than the earlier hearths, and a different shape, and may have served a domestic function. Also, another room, *c.* 6m by 3.5m, was added to the west. It contained a circular clay-lined hearth at its west end, but this may have been replaced by another at the east end where traces of a lightly burnt mortar floor survived, overlying a stone foundation.

most of the buildings continued to be roofed with thatch. A few floor tiles were found, as well as fragments of plain window glass.

Access to the yards and buildings behind the market frontage was also through the alleys, three of which, dating to at least the 14th century, lay within the area excavated; one, in the southernmost property, survived until the Charter Quay development. Such alleys also linked the market to the waterfront, allowing goods to be transported to and from the town centre by boat.

Buildings behind the market frontage were best preserved in the central two of the four properties excavated (corresponding to Nos 7–8 Market Place) (*Fig. 38 & 39*). By the late 15th century these had been extended to the west, although, where walls had been built over the now largely infilled Hogsmill channel, subsidence had caused structural problems. There was no building on the lower lying ground beyond it, and all that was found there were two ditches marking property boundaries, a few gullies and rubbish pits.

The features recorded in northern of the two properties (No 8) illustrate the complexity of the building sequence during this period. Before the 14th century the area to the rear had probably been an open yard, but between *c.* 1400 and 1500 there were three phases of building represented by a succession of walls, hearths or ovens, and floor surfaces. Analysis of the few charred plant remains recovered from the hearths was unable to establish their function, although it is more like-

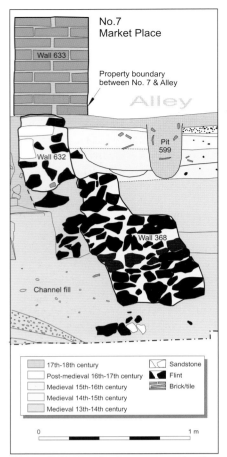

Figure 42: Section showing sequence of walls marking one of the property boundaries in Trench 3.

Legend for Figure 42:
- 17th-18th century
- Post-medieval 16th-17th century
- Medieval 15th-16th century
- Medieval 14th-15th century
- Medieval 13th-14th century
- Sandstone
- Flint
- Brick/tile

ly that they were baking ovens than domestic fireplaces.

The rear of southern property (No 7) also contained substantial buildings of 14th or 15th century date. Apart from a tile-built hearth at No 9 (*Fig. 44*), however, the other two properties (Nos 6 and 9) contained only a number of pits.

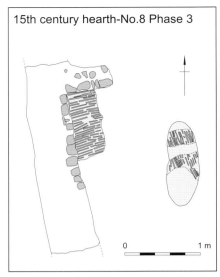

Figure 43: Plan of 15th century hearth.

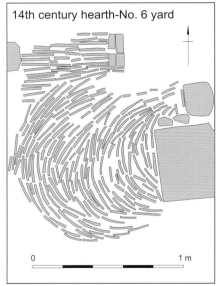

Figure 44: Plan of 14th century hearth.

No 7 Market Place

The rubble foundations of a mid 14th century building c. 6.5m wide but of uncertain length, projected 10m over the (by then infilled) Hogsmill channel, to the rear of the market frontage (*Fig. 42*). Its north wall, marking the property boundary, was traced eastwards for at least 12m, beyond which it had been destroyed by later building. Although the foundations at the western end were c. 1m deep, they did not reach the bottom of the channel and the building had suffered from subsidence at that end. No floor levels, to indicate the building's function, survived, but it may have been used for storage, possibly as a warehouse, or as a workshop.

The building was rebuilt at least once in the late 14th or early 15th century, re-using the earlier foundations on the north side, but extending slightly further to the south and west. There was evidence for at least one internal division, and traces of clay floors survived at the western end. Surprisingly perhaps, the foundations in the second phase were less substantial than those of its predecessor, and it too had suffered from subsidence. It is clear that the walls did not extend to roof height, but instead provided the footings for what was probably a single-storey timber-framed building with panels of wattle and daub infill.

Down Westbitamestrete

As the town around the market developed, so the former suburb of *Clateringbrugende*, south of the Hogsmill, also grew in wealth, stretching further along both sides of *Westbitamestrete* (High Street), and the Charter Quay excavations revealed that during the 14th century the area had a largely industrial character.

In the 19th century 'some beautiful early capitals and bases of piers' of *c*. 1300 date were found near the Guildhall, on land formerly called *La Ryole* (one is now displayed outside Kingston Central Library), pointing to the presence on High Street of a stone building of some importance and architectural merit. Perhaps not coincidentally, there was also a substantial house called *La Ryole* in Vintry Ward (the district of wine importers) in the City of London, and it may be that the same merchant owned both properties. It is known that other important City merchants, including the Lovekyns who were involved in some of the town's inns and wine shops and were buried in All Saints Church, held property in Kingston. They were presumably attracted by the town's location, as both an important local market and as an inland port and transhipment point. Kingston was at the tidal limit of the River Thames, so that while large vessels could sail that far up the river, the presence of the bridge at Kingston would have prevented them from going any further, and their cargoes of wine and other goods would need to be transferred to smaller boats for distribution upstream.

Emms Passage, leading west off High Street, probably became formalised as an alleyway at this time, linking the street and the waterfront, and facilitating the river trade (***Fig. 34***). The limited excavation of the lane near its junction with High Street revealed a sequence of gravel surfaces directly overlying natural deposits.

The absence of later cellars on High Street north of Emms Passage meant that the sequence of 14th to 15th century buildings there was better preserved than on the market place, and medieval deposits lay directly underneath the modern concrete flooring. The late 12th–13th century timber building that had previously occupied this property had apparently long since fallen into disuse, or been dismantled and not replaced. Instead, the property was given over to some form of industrial activity characterised by a series of hearths of varying shape and size (although none closely resembled the keyhole-shaped examples found behind the market place). The presence of similar hearths on the south side of Emms Passage may indicate that the same person owned properties on both sides of the lane. Although documentary study did not uncover the names of

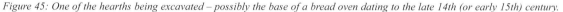

Figure 45: One of the hearths being excavated – possibly the base of a bread oven dating to the late 14th (or early 15th) century.

the 14th century occupiers of the High Street properties, trades there are known to have included iron smithing and possibly gold working. There is no evidence, however, that these hearths were associated with metal working, and baking (*Fig. 45*) or malting are again more likely uses.

By the start of the 15th century the character of the area had changed again, as increasing demand for property led to the division of the earlier single High Street property. The resulting two buildings may have been jettied, although the competition for space in this part of town was still probably less intense than on the market frontage. Both buildings had yards behind them, and a third building, reached from Emms Passage, was built on ground to their rear. This may have been a house, or perhaps a barn or warehouse, with a later northward extension perhaps being used as a workshop or for storage. This may be the building referred to in the 16th century as a barn belonging to one of the properties, probably the southernmost, on High Street.

14th century industrial activity on High Street

The front of the High Street property north of Emms Passage contained a series of pitched-tile hearths, (*Fig.s 48-50*) all within 20m of the street (*Fig. 46*), one dated to *c.* 1375-1400, and its replacement to *c.* 1390-1410. Unlike those behind the market, these were out of doors, although

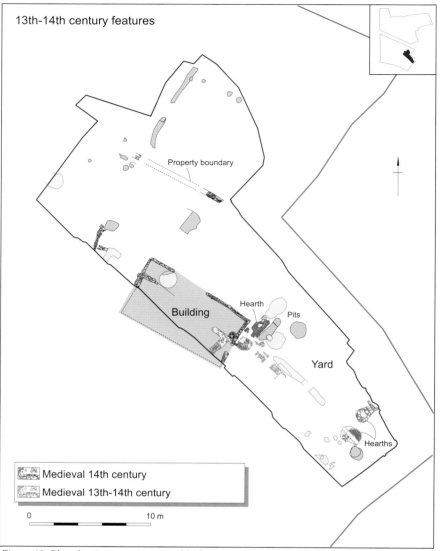

Figure 46: Plan showing concentration of 14th century features near the High Street frontage in Trench 2.

several post-holes near them may indicate the presence of shelters. No clear floors were identified, there being instead a sequence of clay and mortar surfaces interleaved with dark ashy material containing a lot of charcoal. The ground may been of beaten earth strewn with rushes or hay, although as it was probably still prone to periodic flooding, or at least damp, it may have been covered with wooden planking. (A similar sequence of hearths and deposits was recorded in 1990 south of Emms Passage.)

Sometime in the mid-14th century a building, measuring *c.* 9m by 5m, was built to the rear of the hearths, along the north side of Emms Passage. Its eastern end was built over some of the ashy spreads, although it appears to have been broadly contemporary with use of the hearths. It had narrow, low walls that would have provided the footings for a single storey timber frame. There may have been doorways in the east and the south sides, but there were few internal features and the building might best interpreted as a store.

The charred remains of cereals and flower seeds from a pit on the property contained a large quantity of cereal grains, the majority of which were wheat, probably *Triticum aestivum* - a wheat used for making bread. Rye and some barley were also present, along with cornflower and stinking mayweed, both characteristic weeds of medieval crops. Although mixed crops, such as maslin (wheat and rye) and dredge (oats and barley), may have been grown, and mixed grains may have been used for brewing, baking or adding to pottages [18], it was impossible to say whether the grain found had arrived already mixed. The presence of the hearths suggests the grain was used for baking bread for which clean grain would be required.

The remains of beetles recovered from one of the hearths provide further clues as to their use. Although most were from species that infest rotting timber, such as damp flooring, and casks, there were also two grain weevils which feed particularly on wheat and rye. There were also three golden spiders, which eat a wide range of cereals and cereal products, as well as spices and medicinal herbs; they are usually found among vegetable and animal debris in warehouses, poorly kept store rooms and old houses, and although generally regarded as having been introduced into England the 19th century, small numbers may have been introduced earlier.

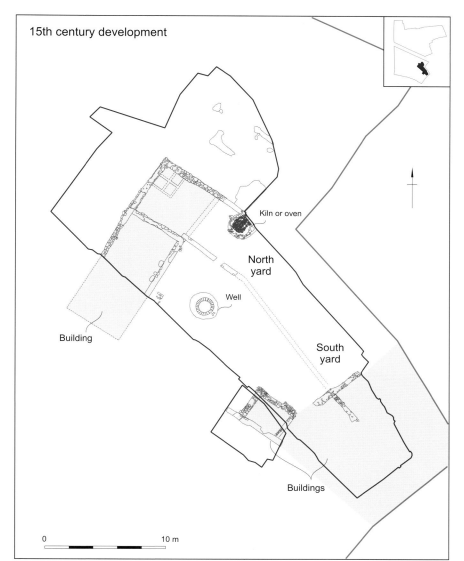

Figure 47: Plan of Trench 2 showing 15th century structural developments.

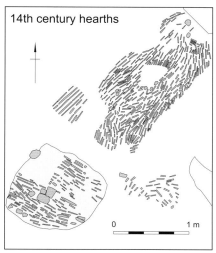

Figure 48: Plan of 14th century hearths.

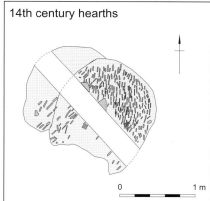

Figure 49: Plan of 14th century hearths.

Property division and construction in the 15th century

At the start of the 15th century, the High Street property on the north side of Emms Lane was divided into two, and two buildings sharing a party wall, each *c.* 12m by 6m, were built aligned at a right angle to High Street (*Fig. 47*). The 14th century building (the possible store) towards the rear of the (now) southern property was initially retained, but then demolished to create a gravel yard opening onto Emms Passage. The yard contained a well, its lower courses formed of squared chalk blocks, the upper part finished in brick (*Fig. 51*). There was a similar yard in the northern property, the two yards being separated by a wall of neatly squared blocks of Reigate stone, forming a simple decorative effect on its south face.

At the same time a new property was laid out to the west, extending from Emms Passage to the Hogsmill, containing a large building, *c.* 10m long and 5m wide, lying at a right angle, and adjacent to, the lane (*Fig. 52*). Like the yard wall (the line of which was continued by the building's north wall) its externally visible walls were made of well-faced chalk and Reigate stone blocks. Its eastern wall butted the remains of the demolished 14th store, and its west wall corresponded approximately with the earlier, but now redundant, 13th century property boundary wall. There was probably a doorway midway along the east side, and traces of a mortar floor and floor joists survived inside. Immediately north of the doorway were three post-holes that may have held posts supporting a second storey.

Around the middle of the 15th century, the building was extended to the north, with a slight change in alignment. The new walls were of a much less regular construction, its east wall being made of quite large, but rather irregular stone blocks, perhaps representing the later blocking of an open-fronted structure. The northwest corner had deeper foundations where it overlay reclaimed land, and here there was a small, shallow, rectangular stone-lined pit divided into four compartments and containing some charcoal – possibly a fuel store.

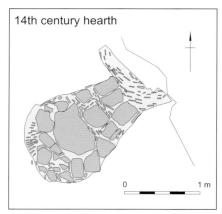

Figure 50: Plan of 14th century hearth.

Figure 52: Foundations and bottom courses of a late 15th century building at 90° to Emms Passage – perhaps a precursor to the later maltings in this property.

Figure 51: Late 15th century well built of chalk blocks and brick located in the yard area.

A small cellar

Behind the High Street buildings, beside Emms Passage, was a small (2m by 3m), 15th century cellar, 1.5m deep (*Fig. 53*). It was built of chalk, Reigate stone and flint with courses of tile, and with mortar on the walls and floor. There were no steps but access would have been from the building above. Charred remains of cereals (mainly wheat), peas and possibly field beans were found in the cellar, but more frequent were items preserved by mineralisation, including apple and grape. Duck and pigeon (probably domestic) were identified in the small quantity of animal bone.

In the material that had been used to backfill the cellar was an iron woodworking axe and a jetton of 15th or 16th century

Figure 53: Late medieval cellared structure adjacent to Emms Passage – a later brick wall lies across the middle. The walls were carefully built of blocks of chalk and Reigate stone interspersed with courses of flint nodules and tile.

date. The jetton (one of three found) originated in France and the Low Countries. Their dating is still uncertain, being issued some time in the 15th or 16th century, although they could have been used up to the 17th century. They were used as reckoning counters, although they also occur on sites where no formal accounting appears to have taken place, and they may have been used as low denomination coins. Seven late 14th or early 15th century pennies were found in a post-hole to the south of Emms Passage, hidden for some reason and never retrieved.

South of Emms Passage there are no medieval buildings later than the 14th century hearths, and the area behind the High Street frontage, which had a series of levelling layers and gravel surfaces, appears to have been used either as yards, or as wharfage where goods were stored. Documents name some of the residents of the area. In 1439, for instance, John and Sylvestra Punche were leased a wedge-shaped strip of waste land along the river on the south side of the Hogsmill adjacent to Clattern Bridge. By 1446, Thomas Broker had 'a garden, a close and a barn' (probably a yard and a warehouse) there, to which a wharf was added by 1455. Immediately to the south of this, by 1440, was a plot called Paradise Garden, which consisted of a two-storey building at the front with a garden behind.

Late medieval trades are known to have included a dyer, a brewer, a boatman and a wood merchant – during the late 13th and 14th centuries, Kingston had become an important centre for stockpiling wood from the surrounding

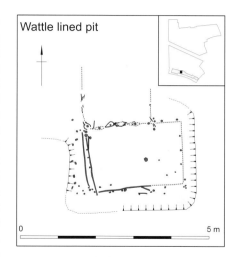

Wattle lined pit

0   5 m

Figure 54: A wattle-lined pit – perhaps a well – dug towards the rear of one of the properties to the south of Emms Passage. A complete horse skeleton was found in the top.

area, before its transport to London in large river boats called 'shouts'. It is possible that a wood merchant held the riverside property (recorded as a woodyard in the 16th century) near the mouth of the Hogsmill, accessed from Emms Passage.

15th century industrial activities

Evidence of industrial activity was found in the yard of the northern of the two High Street properties. The yard surface was made up of several spreads of gravel and other material, including a dump of cattle bucrania – the part of the skull which includes the horn. Two of the skulls had abnormal perforations, which may reflect a pathological response to bearing a yoke across the head. Another deposit contained mainly cattle foot bones. Skull and foot bones are both waste from slaughter, but they may also indicate the processing of hides, as they can be transported to the tannery attached to the skin – the horns effectively acting as 'handles'. (In contrast, a complete horse carcass was found in a wattle-lined pit, infilled in the late 15th century, *c.* 30m from the River Thames (*Fig. 54*). The pit cut a shallow, timber-lined well of 14th–early 15th century date lay, one of very few wells found, perhaps because much of the water used was drawn from the River Thames.)

On the north side of the yard was a length of wall running eastwards from the north-east corner of the extended building to the rear of the property (*Fig. 47*). Built into it was a large kiln or oven (*Fig. 55*). The chamber, on the south side of the wall, was slightly pear-shaped, with a floor of pitched roof tile fragments, and the remains of a clay dome surviving around its edge. The stoke hole was through the wall and a large, shallow, sub-rectangular rake-out pit extended to the north side. Several post-holes and gullies in the vicinity may have formed a shelter to cover the rake-out pit and the surrounding working area.

The rake-out pit contained a lot of charcoal, including both heartwood and sapwood suggesting the use of relatively wide logs (predominantly oak, beech, ash and elm) mixed with narrower roundwood (maple, alder, hazel, blackthorn, birch, willow/poplar). Analysis of the charred plant remains was unable to determine what the kiln was used for – it may have been for malting, a malthouse occupying the site in the 16th century, or for baking, so replacing the series of hearths on the High Street frontage up to the 15th century.

Figure 55: Probable malting kiln. The chamber floor, with the stoke-hole and rake-out pit behind.

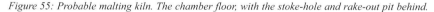

Mills and weirs

There were several weirs in the rivers at Kingston. Thomas Broker held a weir in the Hogsmill in 1417, to the west of Clattern Bridge. No evidence for it was found, probably due to the river's canalisation in the early 20th century. In 1524 there was a weir called *Meydenwer* or Two Mouths, near the Hogs Mill, further upstream. Of particular interest is a reference of 1455 to John Belgeyn having a building in which to keep fish. He may have occupied the property towards the northern end of site, recorded in the 12th–13th century as being occupied by a fishmonger.

Late medieval Kingston had mills at the *Hogs Mill*, and also at *Myddle Mill*, *Chappell Myll* and *Polteresmille*. Mills were also mentioned in connection with the *Saracen's Head* and *George* inns on the west side of the market. It is unlikely they were on these sites, although there is a 16th century reference to 'a garden and a barn in the Back Lane near an old corn mill' at the *George*, and a granary is recorded in the same property at the beginning of the 19th century.

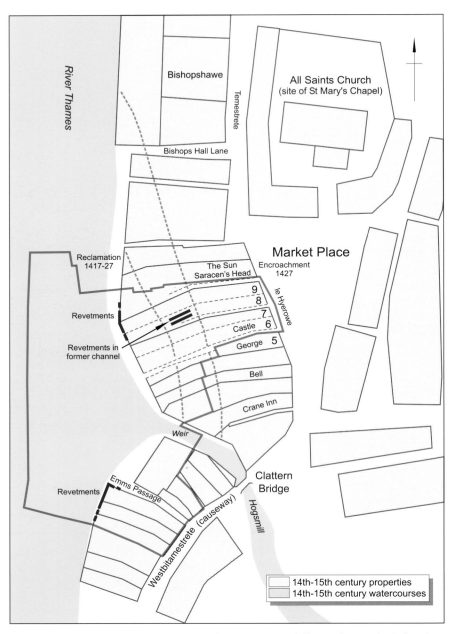

Figure 56: Topography and schematic layout of properties around Charter Quay in the 14th and 15th centuries.

Bridging the Hogsmill channel

As in the 13th century, land was reclaimed within individual properties. At least three more revetments, of probable 14th century date, were found at the rear of the same market frontage property as before (*Fig. 57*), but unlike the earlier revetments, which were aligned north-south along the line of the channel, these ran east-west across it (Fig. 30). As the channel became shallower, the revetments would eventually have blocked it and so provided a 'bridge' across to the low gravel bank to the west, which could itself then be reclaimed. The reclamation of the channel would then have proceeded north and south in the adjacent properties, in due course to the edge of the River Thames and the Hogsmill. These revetments were poorly preserved and less substantial than the earlier examples, reflecting the decreasing depth of the channel as it was filled in. Some of their posts had mortise holes with pegs, indicating the re-use of building timbers (*Fig. 58*). These had been sharpened and driven into the ground to retain the horizontal pieces, of which little survived. The latter were made entirely of sections of planking from the hulls of broken-up boats.

Figure 57: Silty flood deposits interleaved with dumps of gravel and domestic refuse infilling the former channel from the late 13th to early 15th century. Note the remains of three parallel revetments (centre) running across the channel and used to stabilise the infill deposits.

Land reclamation

The pattern of the property boundaries north of the Hogsmill exhibits a curvilinear 'bridgehead' form, which would have given maximum access to both the market and the waterfront (*Fig. 56*). Small changes in alignment of these boundaries, some of which survive today, or are recorded on 19th and 20th century maps, reflect the advances of the properties across the reclaimed ground.

Reclamation of land at the Hogsmill channel had continued through the 14th century, leading eventually to the creation of a land bridge to the gravel bank to its west. A 15th century reference to 'a way for water to go backwards' at the *George* inn may refer to the now blocked channel at the rear of the property, in which water could flow south (i.e. backwards) into the Hogsmill, but no longer north into the River Thames. Also, between the rentals of 1417 and 1427, Richard Est is recorded as having added a 'purpresture' at the River Thames end of his property, to the north of Charter Quay. This may refer to reclamation at the north end of the channel, suggesting that it had now been effectively closed off.

As properties were extended west there were also attempts, in the 14th and 15th centuries, to manage the shores of the River Thames and the Hogsmill in order both to limit the effect of flooding, and also to create wharves which could be reached by lanes running back from the street frontages. The earliest Thames-side revetments in Kingston (recorded in the late 1980s) were found on both sides of the old Kingston bridge, a series of at least six revetments spanning some 200 years from the early 13th to the early 15th century. Some appeared to be purpose-built, made of sawn planks, while others were made of re-used boat and building timbers.

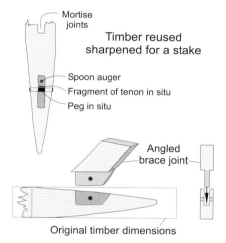

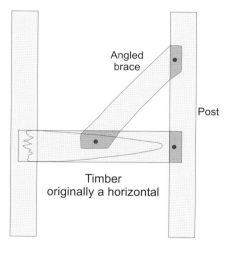

Figure 58: (Top) Building timber reused in revetment. One end has been sharpened to form a stake, but a mortise hole with peg in situ survives. (Bottom) Suggested original position of timber in frame of building.

33

Inns and Industry
The Era of Hampton Court (16th–18th century)

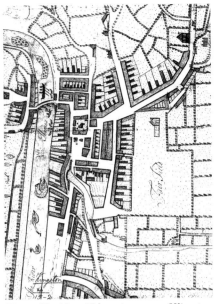

Figure 59: A late 17th century map of Kingston.

Introduction

Kingston continued to expand in the 16th and 17th centuries. At the Hearth Tax assessment of 1664–6 it had 455 households, representing a population of over 2000. A late 17th century map shows the street frontages west of Thames Street, Market Place and High Street as fully built-up, with many buildings stretching behind towards the river (***Fig. 59***).

By 1580 many of Kingston's traders were organised into guilds (woollen drapers, mercers, butchers and shoemakers etc). Trade was uniquely aided by a charter, granted by Charles I in 1628, forbidding the holding of any other market within seven miles. The town became an important centre for brewing, tanning, milling and boat building. Its boats included pinnaces – sea-going vessels which could sail as far as the low arches of the Kingston bridge, goods destined for inland having to be transferred to smaller barges, or to carts for transport overland, or to be sold in the market (***Fig. 60***). The town continued to serve as an inland port throughout the 17th century, the volume of trade being the pretext for the granting in 1662 of a second weekly market day.

Figure 60: Town End Wharf-South of Charter Quay, by H.C. Fox in 1902.

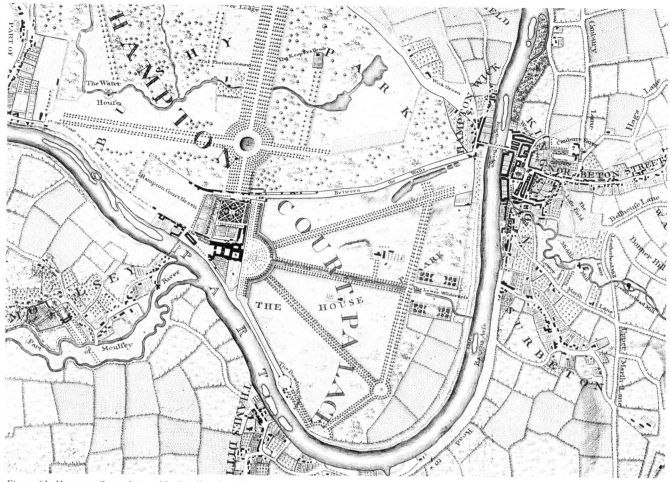

Figure 61: Hampton Court depicted by Knyff in the 17th century.

The town remained virtually free of the bubonic plague that swept England in the 1570s, largely because it banned all people coming from infected areas and established an isolation hospital outside the town. However, when it did succumb in 1625 and 1636, precautions were taken to prevent the disease spreading to the royal residence at Hampton Court across the River Thames (***Fig. 61***). The river traffic of goods to the palace was suspended, and virtually no boats travelled downstream to London.

Beyond that, however, the presence of the palace appears to have had little effect on Kingston's development, although many courtiers stayed in the town, the *Crane* inn on the west side of Market Place being their main lodging place. During the Civil Wars, the town was closely guarded because it held a magazine of arms and ammunition, and a saltpetre works (used for making gunpowder), and because of the bridge which provided a vital Thames crossing. From 1642, control of the town was held by a strong local Puritan clique, and a large detachment of Militia were posted there. In 1647, Sir Thomas Fairfax, Commander of Cromwell's New Model Army, made the *Crane* inn his temporary headquarters. There was no fighting in the town itself, and the main effect of the wars was the cost of billeting soldiers, some of them sick and injured.

Small change

Two farthings of Charles I (1648–1672) were found in a building behind Market Place, in layers contemporary with its floor joists, presumably having been dropped through the floorboards. Two 17th century tokens were also found in this part of the site. One was of Charles Goodwin (vintner) of Barnes, and the other of Thomas Wilmot from 'neare Guildford'. Tokens were issued by individual traders and by civic authorities throughout the country as a response to the shortage and limitations of the small copper farthings originally issued by royal prerogative. Most date from 1648 until the introduction of the copper halfpenny and farthing by Charles II in 1672. Their circulation would not have continued much beyond this date, and geographically they were restricted to the region in which they were issued.

Figure 62: Market Place in 1820, looking south. The Charter Quay site is to the right, then known as High Row.

Most houses in Kingston at the beginning of the 16th century were small. They were usually built of timber frames on stone footings, with wattle and daub infill, some with tiled roofs, but mostly thatched – it was forbidden to burn 'furze bavins' (gorse faggots) for fear of a general conflagration. From the middle of the 16th and into the 17th century there was a phase of rebuilding, with some of the later buildings using brick with timber framing above, and tiled roofs. This coincided with urban rebuilding throughout much of the country at that time, as evident in other Surrey towns, such as along Guildford High Street.

Market Place

The properties at Charter Quay kept their medieval boundaries until the 19th century, although other Market Place and Thames Street properties were further divided and new buildings put up (*Figs 62–5*). Henry Grey, for instance, is recorded as having built four new tenements in Market Place before 1538, and by the mid-17th century the houses there varied in size, having between two and nine hearths. There was also continued encroachment into the market itself. A typical three-storied, double jettied building of this period survives at No 14, at the

market's north-west corner (*Fig. 64*). Documents record that occupations north of the Hogsmill included an apothecary, a tallow-chandler, a shoemaker, a clerk, a joiner, a carpenter, a locksmith, a hardwareman, as well as mercers and watermen.

With the continued reclamation of land at the confluence of the River Thames and Hogsmill there were also lateral divisions to some properties forming tenements to the rear reached through the alleys leading from Market Place. A new building, for instance, was built behind the *Saracen's Head* in 1503. Later, in 1600, a wharf and barn are recorded there.

36

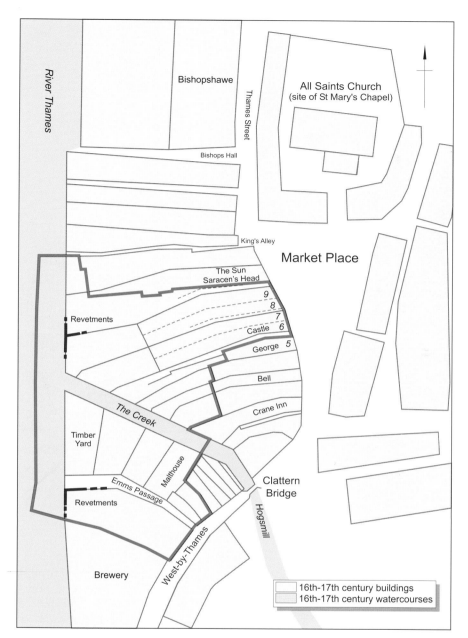

Figure 64: A 16th century timber-framed building (left) in the Market Place, typical of those which once filled the centre of Kingston. The building to the right was re-fronted early in the 20th century in the 'Tudorbethan' style.

Figure 63: Topography and schematic layout of properties around Charter Quay in the 16th and 17th centuries.

Buildings behind Market Place

While the extensive later cellars on the market frontage may have re-used elements of the 16th century buildings, most of the direct building evidence comes from the brick walls, of mainly 17th–early 19th date, of the properties' rear ranges and ancillary buildings, extending west across the infilled Hogsmill channel (*Fig. 65*). Contemporary floor and yard surfaces were generally not well preserved, but the impressions of a series of wooden floor joists survived in a room at the back of one of the buildings (*Fig. 66*).

Open areas became progressively built-up, and although yards and alleys were retained they became increasingly hemmed-in. Some of the building were stables, and parts of seven late medieval or early post-medieval horseshoes were found towards the rear of these properties. There were two brick-lined wells in the most northern of the excavated properties. The earlier had been backfilled in the 17th century while the later, set further back in the property and possibly a replacement, had remained open until the 19th century. In the same property was a carefully built soakaway and a probable cess pit, both built in brick and of probable 17th century date (*Fig. 67*). These structures may reflect an attempt, following outbreaks of plague in 1625 and 1636, to improve sanitation in this crowded part of the town. Previously households would have drawn water directly from the river which was also used for disposing of household refuse and sewage.

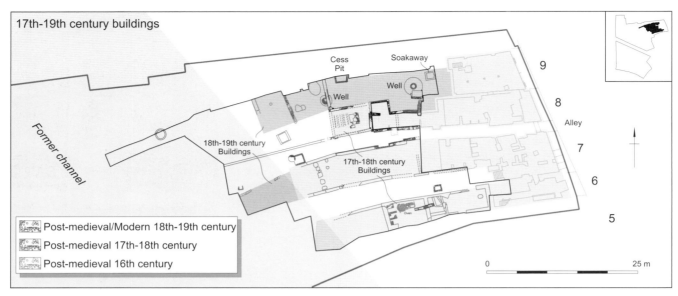

Figure 65: Plan of 17th and 18th buildings found in Trench 3 at Charter Quay.

Figure 66: Impressions of floor joists preserved beneath building.

Figure 67: Brick-lined soakaway. This contained a deposit of animal bones–perhaps waste from tanning or leather working.

Figure 68: Properties along the west side of the Market Place showing inns in existence in the 16th and 17th centuries.

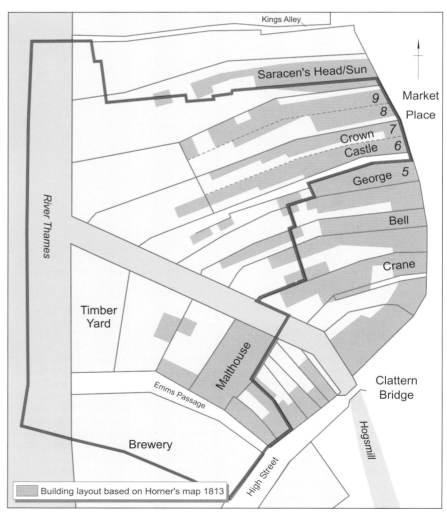

Inns and breweries

Inns were important features of Kingston's market in this period (**Fig. 68**), and three fell wholly or partly within the Charter Quay site. The *Saracen's Head* (later the *Sun*), to the north, and the *George/Castle* to the south, were both established in the late medieval period. Immediately north of the *Castle/George*, the *Crown* was perhaps of 17th century origin, continuing as an inn until the 1760s.

George/Castle

The *George* inn had that name in 1586, but when the property was sold in 1609 it was described as 'formerly used as an inn'. It is probably to be identified with the *Castle* inn, although in the list of Charterhouse properties in 1535, tithes were received from both the *George* inn and the *Castle* inn, suggesting that they co-existed, occupying Nos 5–6 Market Place respectively, until being amalgamated as the *Castle*

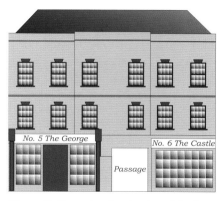

Figure 69: Reconstruction drawing of the front elevation of the Castle inn in the 17th century.

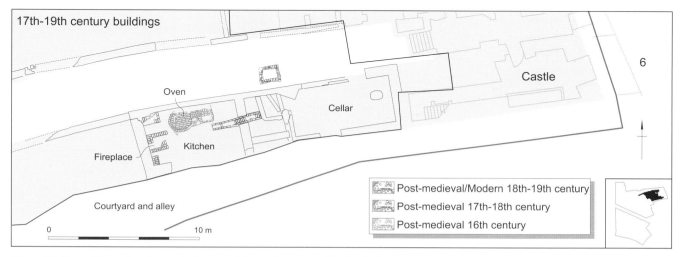

Figure 70: Ground floor plan of range to the rear of the northern part of the Castle Inn.

Castle Inn

Only the northern half of the Castle/George inn lay within the Charter Quay site, but a brick cellar and at least one 17th century room had survived the insertion of later cellars (*Figs 70–2*). The cellar, measuring *c*. 7m by 3.5m, and 1.5m deep with a brick floor, had steps up to the ground floor in its north-west corner (*Fig. 71*). A doorway (later blocked) in the south wall opened onto the alley and small courtyard between the inn's two ranges. On the ground floor a corridor ran north-south, to the west of which was a room, possibly the kitchen, heated by a fireplace at its west end.

Although later rebuilding had removed virtually all traces of the ground, first and second floors, it had, by good fortune, left part of the original roof of the north range behind the Market Place frontage 'marooned' at third floor level (*Fig. 72*).

From the market frontage, a through passage on the right side of the inn's central projecting bay (*Fig. 69*) led back to the rear courtyard. The courtyard was framed on its north side by the panelled facade and hipped roof of the surviving north range (although the render had obscured the surviving wall, the underlying brick fabric was datable to the 17th century). The north range was similar in detail to the inn's former southern range (shown in a historic photograph and described in 1911) suggesting that there had been a uniform architectural treatment on both sides of the courtyard (*Fig 73*). Photographs from 1898 show the initials SB, AB and others, along with a date of 1651, moulded onto the surface of the brick on the south side of the courtyard – the owner of the inn between 1647 and 1664 was Susan Browne. The same initials decorate a fine 17th century staircase from the inn, indicating that both the brickwork and the staircase date to the inn's 1651 rebuild.

The rear of the inn overlay a 16th century brick built oven with a long narrow flue (*Figs 74–6*) and an earlier 14th century hearth. They were probably baking ovens serving the original Castle inn, although the charred plant remains recovered could not confirm this.

Fragments of a small late 16th/early 17th century glass drinking vessel with blown decoration.

in the 17th century (***Fig. 69***). The *Castle* inn, spanning a through passage to the alley and courtyard at the rear, underwent extensive rebuilding in 1651, and its assessment for 27 hearths in 1664 (under the ownership of Susan Browne) suggests it was a large coaching inn. It was one of the earliest, possibly even the first, brick building in the town. Photographs from the late 19th century show a formal, symmetrical façade with a central projecting bay (although by then its 17th century façade had been remodelled with 18th century styling).

An 1803 schedule of the *Castle* inn, gave a full description of the premises and listed its 38 rooms and their fittings, and its outbuildings. The building was rendered at the front, with brickwork at the back, and had a tiled roof with lead gutters. A central gateway with folding gates opened from the rear courtyard onto Market Place. On the north side was a parlour; the bar and bar room probably lay on the south side, with an adjoining room and

Figure 71: Seventeenth century cellar beneath the Castle inn. Note the blocked entrance from the alleyway to the left. The range in the corner to the right is a later insertion blocking an earlier flight of steps.

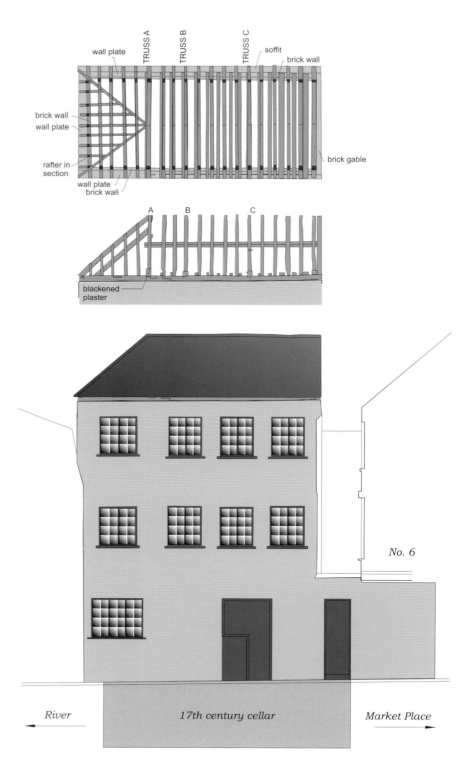

Figure 72: The mid-17th century roof structure survived to the rear of the northern part of the Castle inn.

40

Figure 73: Surviving mid-17th century roof structure to the rear of the northern part of the Castle Inn.

a passage to the rear. Above, on two main floors, were a hall, an Assembly Room, and series of rooms with decorative names like Red Room, Blue Room and White Room, or inn-type names such Spread Eagle, Globe and Boar's Head, including the George – perhaps a reference to the earlier inn. Above them were garrets for servants' accommodation.

On the north side of the yard was a cellar with a tiled and paved floor (this is probably the cellar recorded in the excavation – although the paving had been replaced by brick). It was reached by a stairway from the kitchen, but it also had entrance-flaps from the yard. A doorway led to a separate wine-cellar (the doorway was not identified but probably lay in the east wall, later blocked in). The kitchen was paved with stone, and had a four-shelf dresser and a mantle-shelf (this is probably the room excavated to the west of the cellar).

Also on the north side of the yard were a port-boy room (recently refurbished as a tap room), a laundry (from which a staircase rose), a wash-house paved with brick and stone (with a brick sink and an entry to the pantry), a soldiers' room and an ostlers' room. On the south side of the yard were stables with paved floors, hay-lofts and pantile roofs, a coach-house and a shed for three carriages, two privies, a fowl-

Figure 74: Remains of the 17th century range to the rear of the northern part of the Castle inn. It was built across an earlier oven.

Figure 75: Large piece of gypsum crystal built in to the flue of the oven – was this a good luck charm?

house, and a weather-boarded granary with a tiled roof, raised on stone pillars. (These ancillary buildings are also shown on 19th century maps). At the rear of the premises, beside the Hogsmill, was a fenced garden with vines and fruit trees.

The *Castle* remained in use as an inn until its southern part (No 5) was converted into a shop and dwelling-house before 1837. The northern part continued for some time as the *Castle Tap* inn.

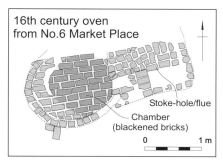

Figure 76: Plan of keyhole-shaped oven, probably a 16th century bread oven.

Figure 77: Late 17th–18th century glass phial fragments.

Figure 78: Complete 18th century wine bottle.

Figure 79: 18th century glass bottle seal.

Figure 80: Mid-17th century staircase from the Castle inn (before renovation).

Figure 82: Finial inscribed with initials.

Figure 83: Carved side panel.

Figure 81: Mid-17th century staircase from the Castle inn (incorporated in new shop).

The Crown

The *Crown* was immediately north of the *Castle*. It was converted in the 1760s to a candlemaker's factory and shop.

Saracen's Head/Sun

The *Saracen's Head* was still called by that name in the 1520s, and is probably to be identified with the *Sun* inn that occupied the site of Nos 10–11 Market Place in the 19th century. A bowling green, adjacent to the River Thames at its rear, appears on maps of the 19th century but may have been established earlier.

Checker/Bell/Lion and Lamb/Druid's Head

To the south of the *George* was the *Bell* (probably formerly the *Checker*), mentioned in 1548, 1572 and 1609. It was later the *Lion and Lamb*, and was called the *Druid's Head* by 1840.

Crane/Bear/Griffin

Further to the south again was the *Crane* inn. This was the most important inn in Kingston in the 16th and 17th centuries, being considered suitable accommodation for the imperial ambassadors in 1526. In 1547 it had an adjacent garden which stretched back to the north shore of the Hogsmill. By 1744 it became the *Bear*, with two stables and common use of a yard. Later, it was renamed the *Griffin*, which in 1835 had stabling for 46 horses, coachhouses and a yard, bars and parlours, cellars and accommodation on two upper floors.

The Market Place inns would have been supplied by the local breweries. South of the Hogsmill, on the site of what is now the *Ram* public house, was a brewery, called the *Berehouse*. It belonged to the Charterhouse estate and was certainly in existence by 1503–4. It was leased out in 1514 with a barn, a garden and all its equipment, which included a 'brass brewing kettle' set in a furnace. In 1527 the tenant

A 17th century staircase

The Castle inn's elaborately carved oak staircase, built *c.* 1651, is documented as having been moved in 1912 when the southern part of the property (No 5 Market Place) became part of a department store (*Figs 80–4*). (Its new position, in No 6, was 50m back from the street frontage, much further back than the extent of any former frontage building). It had square newels covered with rosette and floral motifs, ball finials and a deeply moulded hand-rail. Some finials are inscribed with initials, such as SB for Sarah Browne the inn's owner. The meaning of other initials, in particular IORPGVP, is unclear. The panelled sides have carved scenes with floral rosettes, a seated Bacchus, depictions of brewing, and other images including a symmetrical castle adorned with central and end turrets.

Much of the staircase is of original 17th century date, but some elements, identifiable both in the use of beech and the method of assembly, were introduced when the stair was rebuilt to a reduced scale in 1912. The original staircase was assembled using traditional timber frame methods, while the more recent works used 20th century joinery techniques, such as using nails rather than pegs. It would have been the principal staircase to two or more floors of the Castle inn, but in its rebuilt state it was only used between the department store's ground and first floors. It has now been incorporated in one of the Borders bookshop buildings at Charter Quay.

Figure 84: Bacchus seated on a barrel.

was responsible for the repair of the brewing vessels and the mill there. By 1565, it was leased with a garden, orchard, barn and other buildings to James Norman. However, in the late 16th century, it was greatly expanded by John Rowle (alias Stanton), by the purchase of several houses, buildings and yards, to form a large block of property. Later, in the 17th century, the property was split between various lessees for use as storage and workshops, although there were still granaries on the site.

Another brewer in the area was John Price, who occupied the tenements and yards to the north of Emms Passage. It may have been Price who established a malthouse there during the 16th century, and in 1604 he paid rent for 'a barn and a backside below his house near Clattering Bridge' – that is a warehouse and a yard to the rear of his premises. Several malthouses were established in the area to serve the breweries, and malting became a prosperous trade in Kingston during the 17th and 18th centuries. The large, 17th century brick malthouse to the north of Emms Passage reflects this growth (*Fig. 85*), the building surviving until the start of the 20th century.

Inn food

A bucketful of rubbish dumped over the revetment onto river shoreline behind the Saracen's Head in the late 16th century (*Fig. 90*) gives a unique insight into the food served at the inn.

Meat and fish

There were 122 animal bones, most from immature or very young animals. Such meat, more expensive than other cuts, is highly suitable for roasting and grilling.

The cattle remains represent good quality beef and veal joints. Seven of the eight cattle vertebrae had been axially divided using a heavy cleaver, and eight of the eleven rib fragments had also been chopped, in this case obliquely through the rib shaft. This type of butchery can been seen in rib-steaks and crown – or rib-roast. Poorer quality cuts, as indicated by fragments of shaft common in other cattle bone assemblages and thought to indicate marrow extraction and stews, were absent. Many of the sheep vertebrae had also been axially divided, and the ribs chopped about halfway along, possibly for mutton and lamb chops. Pig was represented by at least two individuals, one a sucking pig a few weeks old, the other a little older.

There were also at least two young rabbits, neither having any visible butchery marks, although such small animals can be prepared, cooked, and eaten without leaving marks. Apart from one from a laying hen, the fowl bones were also from immature birds.

Fish remains included a cod vertebra, chopped laterally – consistent with splitting open the fish for drying, salting, or smoking. (In addition, fishbones recovered from the rear of the Castle inn included plaice, whiting, thornback ray, eel and roach, although herring, commonly found in medieval and post-medieval deposits, were absent. The roach and eel are likely to have been caught locally, but the other, marine species must have been brought to Kingston).

Vegetables

Vegetables included cabbage, and possibly onions, leek or garlic and parsnips. Celery seed may have been used as a spice and parsley as an herb.

Fruit and nuts

Fruit included damson, apple, strawberries and blackberries. The hazelnuts may have been harvested in the country and sold at local markets (large quantities of such nuts were sold in London) or they could have been the improved, larger cultivated type (the filbert), the earliest reference to which is in the Grete Herball of 1526.

Three species are more exotic. The walnut is thought to have been introduced to Britain in the 15th or 16th century, although they were in common use several centuries earlier and may have been grown here earlier. An 11th century Anglo-Saxon glossary includes the name of walnut, 'walsh nutte', meaning the nut from foreign lands (usually France or Italy). Accounts for the Holborn gardens of the Earl of Lincoln in 1295–6 include an entry for £9 for pears, apples and 'great nuts' (walnuts) sold from the garden. Their culinary uses in fruit pies and sweet and sour meat dishes are described in two cook books of 1430. Later sources, such as the *Holinshed Chronicles* of 1580, included walnuts among new varieties imported within the previous 40 years, in comparison with which the old trees were judged to be worthless.

Tradition holds that fig trees were introduced by Pole, later to become Cardinal, and planted in the gardens of Lambeth Palace in 1525. According to an early 18th century writer, the trees, of the White Marseilles variety often considered to be the most delicious in cultivation, were still growing two centuries later. It is likely, however, that the figs seeds from Charter Quay were from imported, dried fruit. The grapes, also, whose pips were found in the deposit, were probably imported and eaten as raisins – the *Holinshed Chronicles* of 1580 mentions that vineyards had almost disappeared from Britain.

This is the waste of a high quality meal, and it is reflected in the remains of at least four late 16th or early 17th century glass vessels from the same deposit. Three are small drinking vessels (beakers) with mould-blown 'wrythen' decoration of *façon de Venise* type, and the fourth is a small jar or beaker with plain flared rim. Beakers with 'wrythen' decoration, along with other *façon de Venise* vessels, were produced in the Netherlands, but also copied by the English glasshouses of the period, such as Hutton and Rosedale [19]. They are found in the major south coast ports such as Plymouth and Exeter [20]. A fifth drinking vessel, represented by the footring from a stemmed goblet from a dump layer in a property to the south-east, is less closely dated to the 16th–17th century.

A hangover remedy?

Six seeds of feverfew, or batchelor's buttons, were recovered from the rubbish deposit. The species, common today, arrived in Britain during the medieval period. As its name suggests, it has been used to treat many ailments including colds and fevers, and was the equivalent of today's aspirin, recommended for migraine, headaches, rheumatism and general aches and pains. The seeds may have come from a plant growing in the garden of the inn, but given its restorative properties it may also have been used to help alleviate the over-indulgence of the inn's customers!

There is also a suggestion that strewing herbs were used in the inn to mask unpleasant smells. Amongst the plant material in the deposit (which included wheat and rye stems and roots, a number of grassland plants possibly the remains of hay, as well as bracken and heath grass, much of it probably the remains of straw used for flooring) were several species of 'weed', including meadowsweet and sweet violet.

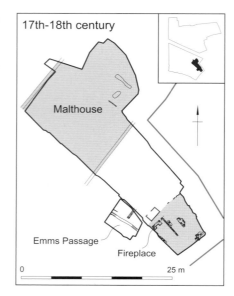

Figure 85: Plan of 17th and 18th buildings found in Trench 2 at Charter Quay.

Figure 86: A 16th-17th century timber-framed building which stood on the corner of the High Street and Emms Passage until the 1960s.

In 1672, Stephen Feild and Francis Houlden bought a malthouse at the south end of Clattern Bridge from Robert Pike, and ran it as partners. This is almost certainly the malthouse that stood on High Street just south of Charter Quay (*Fig. 87*). A malthouse was working here until 1895, later turned into a furniture shop called 'Ye Olde Malte House'. It was a conspicuous landmark, its round chimney had a large vent on the top, but was illegally demolished shortly after being given a preservation order in 1965.

Rebuilding along Emms Passage

In the 17th century a cobbled surface was laid over the medieval and early post-medieval gravel surfaces in Emms Passage. On its north side, while only fragmentary structural remains survived on the High Street frontage, parts of the brick footings of the south and west walls, and the north party wall, of a 16th century timber-framed building were recorded (*Fig. 85*). They had been built partly on the foundations of the earlier stone buildings. (The eastern wall lay outside the limits of excavation, beneath the modern pavement). Inside, was the base of a large brick fireplace and chimney stack, and a narrow brick wall which may have supported joists for a timber floor. Other brick walls to the rear indicate a range extending alongside Emms Passage, probably demolished and replaced in the 19th century.

This building stood until the late 1960s, when it was demolished. A photograph (*c.* 1965) shows that it was two storeys high (like several others of the same period in this area), and jettied at first floor level on its High Street and Emms Passage frontages (*Fig. 86*). A later mansard roof (having a two slopes, the lower one steeper), most likely of 18th century date, had windows to an attic. A brick facade was probably added to the High Street frontage at the same time – a common device to give an older building a more modern appearance.

Similar buildings probably stood in the property to the north, and also in the two properties south of Emms Passage. However, apart from fragmentary remains of brick walls, a brick-floored cellar of 18th or 19th century date and limited photographic evidence, there is little surviving evidence mainly because of damage caused by the building of a cinema in the 20th century. The cellar, south of Emms Passage, contained some re-used Reigate stone, and in the rubble backfill were several pieces of intricately carved and scorched stone, perhaps from the building to which the cellar belonged, or from an earlier structure.

To the west, however, there were substantial remains of a mid–17th century brick malthouse. This replaced the earlier stone building which had stood there (possibly an earlier malthouse), but now covered a much larger area, extending from Emms Passage to the Hogsmill, as well as further north-west, and also cutting off the ends of the properties to the south-east. No floors or internal features survived, these probably having been removed during the building's conversion to a garage at the beginning of the 20th century.

Other than these structural remains there were few other post-medieval features north of Emms Passage, and very little pottery or other finds to attest to the intensity of use of the site. However, several 16th–18th century pits, and a variety of 17th–18th century dumps and make-up layers, including much redeposited gravel, were recorded south of Emms Passage. This suggests that large areas at the rear of the High Street properties here remained as open ground used for rubbish disposal, perhaps until the middle of the 19th century when the southern frontage of Emms Passage was built-up.

Excavations in 1979 at Nos 15–17 High Street, immediately to the south-east and on the opposite side of the street to Charter Quay, revealed the base of a large, circular oven approximately 2m in diameter which had been rebuilt at least once. This has been provisionally dated to the late 16th century, although its function is unknown; it may possibly have been a baker's oven or perhaps associated with malting or brewing.

Businesses south of the Hogsmill in the 16th and 17th centuries are known to have included shoemakers, a tailor, a linen draper, a mercer, a butcher, a poulterer, a wharf-owner, brewers, coopers, wheelwrights and mealmen, while increasingly important were the carpenters, joiners and wood merchants who operated the timber yards.

The period saw continued development and rebuilding, processes reflected in contemporary documents, such as the 1545 lease to Thomas Robinson of a strip of waste land along the east side of West-by-Thames Street (High Street) to build the frontage of new tenements. In 1548, Martyn James, who leased a tenement by Clattern Bridge (probably Nos 16–18 High Street, adjacent to the properties excavated at Charter Quay) was required to build a 'good and meet kitchen' at least 10ft by 20ft (3m by 6m) at its rear. Later, in his lease of 1565, he was required within six years to rebuild the

tenement, now divided into two houses; by 1666, it had been divided into three dwelling-houses. Also in 1565, James Norman was required to repair the brewery and build a new barn, a short distance to the south of Charter Quay. By 1609 William Young had built a house, a barn and other buildings at the edge of town in West-by-Thames Street. In 1700, the Thrustly family's property at Nos 12–14 High Street, adjacent to the Clattern Bridge, consisted of two two-storey houses, with garrets above, cellars below and shops in the front.

Following Queen Elizabeth's donation in 1564 of the Charterhouse estate to endow Kingston's Grammer School, rents, including those from the property excavated to the north of Emms Passage, the brewery further to the south, and the *George* inn on the market frontage, were paid towards the school's support.

Some of the tenants in the area south of the Hogsmill were fishermen. Eels were caught each year at the Eel Fair in mid-May, when the young eels migrated up the River Thames. There were still weirs in the rivers, and Queen Mary had granted the town the right to make a weir in the River Thames in 1556, together with the rents of two other fish weirs. There were also weirs in the Hogsmill, including the late medieval weir to the west of Clattern Bridge formerly operated by Thomas Broker, owned by Audemer and worked by Richard Standon in 1503.

There were major floods in Kingston in October 1570, and again *c.* 1777 when the River Thames rose so high that it was possible to row boats into Market Place. In the winter of 1588–9 John Davyson was paid for a boat to find timbers carried away by a flood, and for breaking ice at the Kingston bridge. In February 1795 a sudden

Figure 87: Former maltings (centre) which stood in the High Street south of Charter Quay until demolished in the 1960s.

45

Figure 88: Flooding in the High Street in 1895.

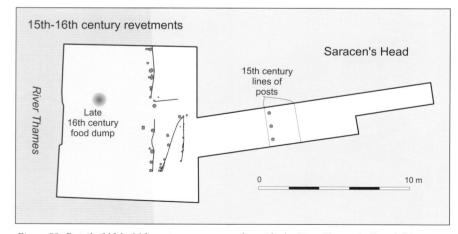

Figure 89: Sequence of 15th–16th century revetments alongside the River Thames in Trench 34.

Figure 90: Detail of 15th–16th century revetments alongside the River Thames in Trench 34.

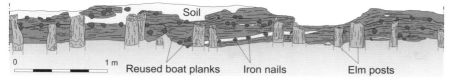

15th-16th century revetment elevation

Soil

0   1 m   Reused boat planks   Iron nails   Elm posts

Figure 91: Elevation drawing of part of a 16th century revetment constructed from re-used boat timbers [after DGLA].

thaw caused another flood which damaged warehouses in the town, and drainage remained a problem in the centre of Kingston during the 19th century (***Fig. 88***). Continuing efforts were made, therefore, to manage the rivers and defend against floods, and there was further reclamation of land, particularly north of the Hogsmill.

Wharves, revetments and the Hogsmill development

The former Hogsmill channel was finally filled in at the beginning of this period, a mid 16th century document referring to the closure of its northern end. In 1563 John Jenyns was leased a piece of land at the Thames end of Bishop's Hall Lane with 50ft (15m) of a drainage channel (called the Creek) that he was required to fill and level whilst maintaining a watercourse draining water from Thames Street into the river.

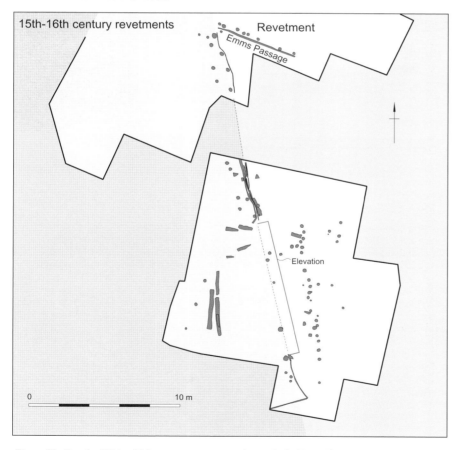

15th-16th century revetments   Revetment

Emms Passage

Elevation

0   10 m

Figure 92: Detail of 15th - 16th century revetments alongside the River Thames in Trench 1A.

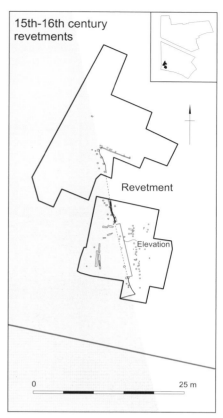

15th-16th century revetments

Revetment

Elevation

0   25 m

Figure 93: 15th–16th century revetments alongside the River Thames in Trench 1A.

Traces of revetments incorporating re-used boat timbers were found on the River Thames shore at the rear of the *Saracen's Head* inn, and on properties to the south. Similar revetments were recorded south of Emms Passage, one of which 'returned' at a sharp angle along the line of the lane, which was extended westwards as land was reclaimed, a process reflected in slight kinks in its line. Documents record that, by 1565, the bank of the River Thames south of Charter Quay was protected by a stone wall.

It is unclear to what extent the banks of the Hogsmill were revetted during the 16th and 17th centuries.

Excavation in 1979 to the southeast of Clattern Bridge, behind Nos 15–17 High Street, revealed a wattle revetment along the river side, but excavations west of the bridge revealed on its south side only reclaimed land overlying alluvial deposits.

47

Unlike the revetments that were built to stabilise the riverbanks, the creation of wharfs reflects the use of the waterfront for trade, and indicates the likely presence of yards, warehouses and other storage and industrial buildings. Documents refer to wharfs north of the Hogsmill from the 16th century – the innkeeper of the *George* inn is recorded as having paid rent for a barn and a

Figure 95: Engraving by J.Greig showing reused timbers in the revetment north of the Hogsmill.

Figure 96: Deck planking from a boat.

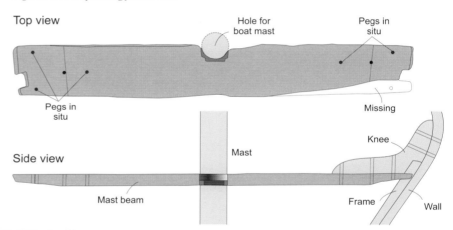

Figure 94: Part of the deck planking from a boat. This unusual piece includes one half of the mast step shown in detail here.

Land reclamation

Some idea of the condition of the River Thames in the 16th century can be gained from the waterlogged plant remains found at the rear of the *Saracen's Head*. The presence of species such the fringed waterlily (only native in the Thames valley and East Anglia), water-plantain, horned pondweed and branched bur-reed, suggest that the river was slow moving and possibly brackish. All are capable of withstanding some degree of organic enrichment, which was probably increasing due to the dumping of household waste and raw sewage directly into the river.

The 15th century pile revetments found north of the Hogsmill were superseded in the 16th century by two revetments further to the west, incorporating re-used boat timbers held in place by sharpened elm posts (*Figs 90 & 95*). The revetments were in two adjoining properties, the northern property (belonging to the *Saracen's Head* inn) containing only one revetment, while that to the south had a sequence of three. Further revetments with re-used boat timbers were found north of the Hogsmill during 1988, but none was particularly substantial.

No waterfront revetments were found around the mouth of the Hogsmill later than the early 16th century, but these may have been located closer to the River Thames. There was, however, extensive dumping of soil and rubbish from the 16th–18th century, raising the ground level by up to 1m in places. These dumps, which overlay the earlier revetments, included large quantities of clay pipes (most within the date range 1640–1680) and vessel glass of later 17th-18th century date. South of the Hogsmill, as far as Emms Passage, there was an expanse of alluvial deposits and intertidal muds, indicating that this area still had not been reclaimed.

To the south of the Emms Passage, the 15th century pile revetments were superseded by three further revetments, set 10–15m back from the current waterfront, one forming the corner of the property and turning at a sharp angle along the line of lane. Their skewed angle relative to the present riverbank suggests that the river had formerly swung further to the east at this point. Here also the revetments incorporated boat timbers and elm posts, the ground behind them (which were probably no more than 0.5m high) being built up with gravel, domestic refuse and any soil that was available. (*Figs 93*).

Figure 97: 16th and 17th century revetments in Trench 1a prior to excavation.

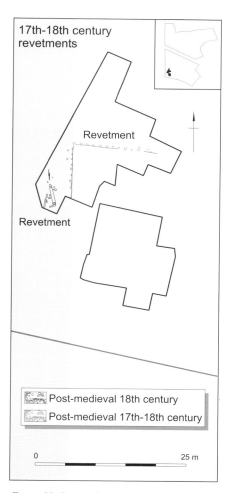

17th-18th century revetments

Revetment

Revetment

Post-medieval 18th century

Post-medieval 17th-18th century

0   25 m

Figure 98: Post and plank revetment of probable 17th century date and 18th century 'floating revetment', alongside the River Thames in Trench 1A.

wharf in 1503–4, although no traces of these were found, and there continued to be a wharf to the rear of the inn in 1609–11, with a lane on its south side and another wharf to its north. The plot on the east side of the *Crane* inn's garden was described as a shore in 1537, but as a wharf by 1553.

A wharf on the south bank of the Hogsmill was recorded in 1597 as needing repair and additional wharfing. Although this would have lain on the north edge of the southern excavated area, no traces survived the later canalisation of the river. A 7ft (2.13m) wide passage was made running northwards to the wharf in 1609, surviving until the 1960s. There was also a wharf adjacent to the west side of Clattern Bridge in 1700 (referred to in 1903 as Clattern Wharf. By 1738, the north side of the river adjacent to Clattern Bridge was lined by a brick wall thirteen inches (0.33m) thick, adjoining the *campshot* (piles and boarding) of the river mouth.

The best preserved sections of boat were *c.* 1.5m long and up to four planks high (*Fig. 91*). The planks were held together with large iron rivets, and where they overlapped (being 'clinker-built') they were packed with animal hair. Hair and wool were used to provide a watertight joint even in the largest medieval ships, cattle hair being most common in the 12th century, goat hair in the 14th and 15th centuries, and wool in the 16th century.

One timber from the revetment differed from the hull sections. It was a mast beam, *c.* 3.5m long spanning the boat, with a semi-circular cut (with a square rebate below) in the centre of one edge to hold a mast, perhaps 0.3m in diameter (*Fig. 94 & 96*). The ends of the plank had been chamfered and notched to fit over the frame of the boat, and the holes at either end are where the 'knees' joined the beam to the hull. On the basis of this timber, the boat would have been at least 3.5m wide, with a mast that could probably be removed or folded down, suggesting a substantial river vessel able to pass under the Kingston bridge, possibly one used in transporting goods down river, to and from Kingston.

A later revetment at this point (*Fig. 97*), probably of 17th century date, was of post and plank construction. Unlike the earlier revetments, it was purpose-built, containing no re-used building or boat timbers. It consisted of one or two surviving 'courses' of sawn oak planks laid horizontally and held in place by regularly spaced, squared oak posts (*Fig. 95*). Like one of the earlier revetments, it also turned along the line of lane, but now at 90° angle reflecting a change in the alignment of the riverbank (*Fig. 98*). One later 'floating revetment' (*Fig. 99*), of quite different construction, may have been of 18th century date. Only a small part of it was exposed, but it consisted of a substantial square-sectioned, possibly re-used, timber with large mortise holes at either end through which posts had been driven to hold it in place. Rather than a revetment stabilising the riverbank it may have been used to berth boats against.

To the south of the Hogsmill, documents record a wharf facing the River Thames by 1567, served by a lane on the line of Emms Passage (probably called Thurrocks Lane). It was used as a timber wharf by John Whyte, and later, in 1600, by John Rowle (alias Stanton) who, in 1581 and 1583, had provided planks and other timber for the repair of the Kingston bridge. No trace of any revetments were found in the excavations of this area which consisted entirely of alluvial deposits thinning out to the south-west, and it is possible that timber was simply stored here on the gently sloping shoreline.

In the early 17th century wharfage extended rapidly southwards along High Street. Wharves were built by William Young by 1608, by Thomas Blackfan on the plot to the south in c. 1617, and by John Mudgett on the next plot in 1653. Several of these wharves were also used as timber yards, and at others imported coal was stored in sheds. Further to the south still, the brewery had a wharf by 1619–22, with river stairs where corn was unloaded, and a privy at the waterside. By 1695, the River Thames shore was protected by a brick *rampier* on stone arches – a lease of 1716 noted possible damage to the *rampier* by floods or by ice coming down the river. However, no stone or brick walls were found in the excavations, although these may have lain closer to the river.

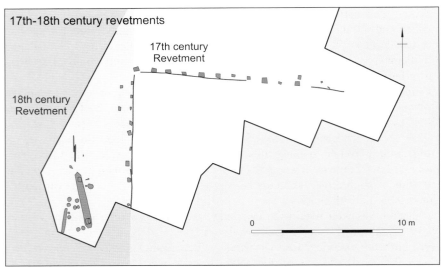

Figure 99: Detail of 17th century post and plank revetment and 18th century 'floating revetment'.

Trade and industry

Seventeenth century Kingston contained maltings and brewhouses, forges, timber yards and a brick yard, and slaughter houses and tan yards. There were also the sheds of carpenters, masons, chandlers and weavers. Many of these activities would have been reflected in the town's waterborne trade and some continued well into the 20th century (*Fig. 100*).

Bone filled pits on properties west of Market Place point to animal processing, in particular the skinning, dismembering and disposal of horse carcasses. These may have been purchased by a knacker or fellmonger from the local horsefair north of Market Place, who sold on the hides on to the tanner or *whittawyer*. These rather smelly processes would probably not have been welcome in high status areas, or close to the market. From the 16th century onwards the west side of the town may have become a specialist area for tanning and related industries, because of its ready supply of water. A skinner is recorded in the area in the 14th century, and there was a tannery at Bishops Hall to the north of the site by 1723. This developed into Kingston's largest and most important tannery, operating on the same site until its closure in 1963.

Figure 100: Timber yards, maltings and breweries north of Kingston Bridge at the end of the 19th century.

Within the Charter Quay site, Robert Ranyard and his family began, in 1762, making and selling their famous Kingston Candles, rushlights and tallow dips at the candle-maker's factory and shop on the site of the former *Crown* inn. Candlemaking, like tanning, was a malodorous process and involved melting down fat from offal and mutton to make tallow.

Unlike in the medieval period, when most livestock would have been supplied from the local area, there was now more long distance trade, beef being driven from as far away as Scotland to be fattened in East Anglia and the Home Counties before delivery to London. Some of the cattle bone from the pits may have come from animals brought to Kingston's livestock market, to be sold, slaughtered and processed before the meat was sent to London. There was a slaughterhouse on the east side of High Street while the houses opposite (Nos 16–18) were owned by butchers in the 17th century.

Kingston was well within the catchment area that provided London, via the River Thames, with wood and charcoal [21], and most woodlands around the town were probably exploited for this lucrative fuel trade. There was evidence of a charcoal store behind one of the market place properties, possibly providing a link with *le coliere* (charcoal supplier) recorded earlier in this area.

Charcoal

A large spread of charcoal in the property north of the Castle inn may have been the remains of a charcoal fuel store (rather than wood fuel debris from, for example, bakers' ovens), with several postholes in the area possibly supporting a shelter over it. Charcoal burns at high temperatures and although it was important for metal-working (prior to the use of coal), there was no evidence of this on the site. It is more likely to have been used in domestic braziers for heating, in common with London practices.

The charcoal consisted of narrow round-wood (i.e. small branches and twigs of oak, alder, birch, hazel, willow/poplar, ash and holly), that would have been cropped, following the traditional pattern of felling, during the dormant season. The growth patterns indicate a high ratio of coppice wood, grown on rotational cycles of up to 15 years, the oak being cropped on a cycle of up to 10 years.

Animal processing

A number of early 17th century pits sited near the river, from a property south of the *Saracen's Head* inn, were filled with tightly packed animal bone, probably reflecting the processing of animal carcasses. The pits were *c*. 1m in diameter and up to 1m deep, and one that was fully excavated produced 667 individually identifiable bones. Horse was most common (417 bones) then cattle, with sheep, pig, roe and fallow deer also being repre-sented. It is likely that the other pits, the surfaces of which had similar bones, were filled at the same time.

The remains of at least 11 horses were recovered, and they had, to a greater or lesser degree, been processed. There was evidence of skinning, disarticulation and at least some meat removal, and it is likely that the tails were removed with the skin, as horsehair had a variety of uses. The bones, however, had not been chopped and split as is normal for the removal of meat and marrow from cattle bones. They were little damaged and were probably disposed of rapidly, unlike other material from the pits which displayed evidence of having been gnawed and eroded, and may have been left lying around for some time before being buried.

Dumps of horse bone have been found on several earlier excavations in Kingston, such as a group of at least 12 horses found at Eden Walk in the 1980s, although these were of late 14th century date. Like these, the horses at Charter Quay were generally mature or even old. There was a single animal aged between one year and 18 months, but the remainder included one female aged about 10 years, three males aged about 15–16 years, one about 18–19 years and two over 20 years, one of which was extremely old. As at most medieval and post-medieval sites, the horse remains at Charter Quay are consis-tently of older or diseased animals, presumably at the ends of their useful lives (*Fig. 101*). The one younger horse appears to have had some disease. Horsemeat was not usually intended for human consumption, but those horses no longer fit for work through age or disease would still provide hide, hair and glue.

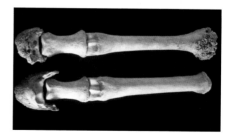

Figure 101: Medieval horse bones. Compare the diseased and healthy leg bones.

The withers heights of the horses ranged from 1.24m to 1.50, with more than half over 1.4m (roughly 14 hands). This contrasts with the earlier examples from Eden Walk, which ranged from 1.19m to 1.43m, only two being over 1.4m, a range more typical for medieval hors-es. Today, anything under 14.2 hands is classified as a pony, although this does not mean that smaller animals cannot carry a heavy per-son or pack. The majority of medieval horses seem to have been pony-sized, but improvements were encouraged by Henry VIII's 1537 requirement that landowners keep mares of 13 hands and over, followed by an Act of 1541 requiring stallions to be 15 hands and over.

Old plough oxen would have been more valuable than old horses because they could be fattened up for slaughter. The cattle bones from these pits, unlike those from Eden Walk, included no groups of cattle horn cores, often an indication of tannery waste, although it seems most probable that the animals had been skinned for their hides.

Figure 102: Buildings at Nos 26–28 High Street, south of Emms Passage, in 1897.

Figure 103: Medieval and Post-medieval pottery, clay pipes and a drop handle.

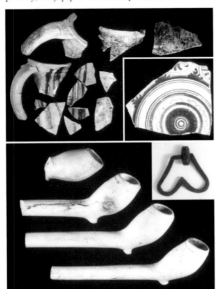

Pottery and other finds

There was very little pottery from Charter Quay that can be dated to later than the 17th century (*Fig.103*). Most were coarse earthenwares – largely redwares, but with some whitewares from the Border Ware industry. Some of the redwares may have been locally made, small-scale production being indicated by a late 15th–early 16th century dump of wasters behind Nos 15–17 High Street [22]. This site lay immediately southeast of Charter Quay, on the opposite side of the street, and although no kiln was found it is suspected to have been at the rear of No 17. Some 45kg of pottery, from at least 60 vessels, were recovered. Other potential redware sources include the Border Ware industry and various kilns in south London. Other wares occurred in very small quantities and included German and English stonewares, tin-glazed earthenwares and Staffordshire-type slipwares.

The pottery was almost exclusively utilitarian, with very few finewares. Exotica were limited to a single sherd from a Spanish olive jar and two sherds from a North Italian marbled slipware bowl. There was little here to reflect Kingston's role as an inland port, nor are there any specialised forms related to specific craft or industrial functions.

Numerous copper alloy pins were found, particularly in the properties west of Market Place. Most are the short, post-medieval types often associated with dressmaking, although longer, globular-headed examples are present. A group of cattle and horse foot bones, found in a well south of the *Saracen's Head* inn, included several that had been whittled to a point at one end, possibly representing unused pinners' bones - bones shaped to hold copper alloy pins (mainly used as clothes fasteners) while their points were filed during manufacture.

The rest of the copper alloy assemblage included little of functional significance for the site. Personal items were the most common – five buckles, four lace tags and one hooked tag, all of 15th–17th century date. Other identifiable objects included two thimbles, a cast vessel fragment and a heart-shaped drop handle, probably from furniture; again, these are likely to be late medieval or early post-medieval date. A small carved bone dice could have come from one of the inns.

52

Figure 104: The Odeon cinema at Nos 25-28 High Street.

19th–20th century developments south of the Hogsmill

In 1831, Clattern Bridge was still only 8ft (2.44m) wide. However, it was subsequently widened twice, the second time, on its eastern side, in 1852. Around 1900, the Hogsmill to the west of the bridge was canalised in its present course, and it now flows in a concrete-lined channel.

Some properties within the Charter Quay site south of the Hogsmill are shown on a sale plan of 1851, and the whole area north and south of the Hogsmill is depicted in some detail on the Goad Fire Insurance Map of 1907, which shows the various uses of the buildings at the time. North of Emms Passage, on the site of the former timber yard, was the premises of one Kingston's famous boat building firms, Burgoigne's, established in the 1860s. Burgoigne's continued in business until 1910, after which the site remained as a boatyard, but was also used in the 1920s and 1930s as a bathing site.

The 17th century malthouse which stood to the east had been demolished and replaced, by 1907, by a motor garage, but the 16th century timber-framed building at the corner of the High Street and Emms Passage survived until the 1960s. South of Emms Passage, within the Charter Quay site, were four High Street

A set of false teeth

Perhaps the most intriguing, and certainly the most personal object from the Charter Quay, proved to be a set of false teeth, or rather a partial upper plate with a single tooth attached, found in a brick-lined feature towards the rear of Nos 8–9 Market Place. The plate is made of gold, carefully gum-moulded to fit around existing teeth, and the single tooth, attached on one side with a gold rivet, is of porcelain; there are traces of a second attachment on the opposite side. The plate would have been very close-fitting (*Fig. 105*).

It is likely to date from the early 19th century. William IV (1830–1837) apparently wore a gold upper plate with carved ivory teeth [23], and a plate similar to the Charter Quay example, also with porcelain teeth, was found in the crypt at Christ Church, Spitalfields, fitted into the mouth of William Leschallas, who shot himself in 1852 [24]. Such items, and others from the Spitalfields crypt, are likely to have belonged to fairly wealthy individuals.

properties including George Bennett's linen drapery at Nos 28–30 (*Fig. 102*), and a hairdressers and theatrical wig maker at No 26. These buildings, which appear from a photograph to have been of late 17th or 18th century date, were subsequently demolished and replaced by an Odeon cinema (*Fig. 104*). This in turn has been demolished and will provide the site for a new theatre to form part of the Charter Quay development.

Figure 105: Early 19th century gold denture.

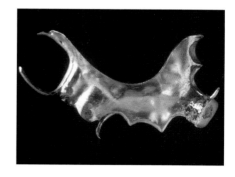

The History of the Buildings
at Cardinal's Department Store, Market Place

The Cardinal's department store building at Nos 6–9 Market Place was the end product of a process of redevelopment starting in the late medieval period, and its recording before demolition in 1999 was an integral part of the archaeological work at Charter Quay (*Fig. 106*). Preserved in its structure were elements from key phases of its complex history, including those for which it had been assigned a statutory listing:

• the 17th–20th century cellars covering the full width of the property's Market Place frontage

• an elaborately carved mid–17th century timber staircase (originally from No 5)

• a small 17th century range set back from the street on the south side (No 6), with a tiled, hipped roof and panelled elevation

Figure 106: Extract from Rowlandson's drawing of the Market Place dated c. 1800.

Nos 6–9 Market Place, as the property's address implies, had formerly been four individual adjacent properties on the western side of the market place (No 6 to the south). Although occupation of the site began in the 12th century, there was no standing building fabric that could be dated to earlier than the 17th century. Medieval property boundaries, once defined, often persisted for a long time, and although Nos 6–9 became a single property in

The cellars

All the cellar spaces below the frontages of Nos 6–9 Market Place were interconnected, but each differed (*Fig. 107*). The southern two cellars, at Nos 6–7, consisted of a number of discrete spaces with arched side niches, while those at Nos 8–9 comprised larger open spaces. A narrow link between the cellars of Nos 7 and 8 marked the line of the ground floor level through passage to the alley behind. This would have provided access to rooms further back, internal courtyards and the rear of the property.

The cellars would probably have had vaulted ceilings supported on square sectioned piers, but any evidence of the ceilings had been removed (at a height of c. 1.5m) by the insertion of a modern concrete ground floor in 1912. All the cellars appeared to consist of a main area situated toward the frontage, with other rooms of varying size and form extending back into their plots. There was evidence of former light wells along the front of all the properties, suggesting that the frontages had advanced slightly into Market Place over the years.

The earliest evidence of access to the southern cellars area consisted of a flight of eight brick and timber steps in No 7, the walls flanking them being were datable to the 18th and 19th centuries, and so contemporary with the creation of the bank registered at No 7 from 1792. The cellars were later reached by a new stairway built against the south side of No 6 with trap door access, and by wooden stairs to the north, in No 9.

The different floor surfaces in each cellar illustrate the former autonomy of each property, as well as the variety of their uses. The floor in No 6 was mainly brick, while those in Nos 7 and 8 were a mix of brick, tile and concrete. The floor in No 9 was quite different, consisting of distinctive square ceramic tiles and small areas of earlier brick laid perpendicular to the side walls, with sunken stone pillar bases aligned off centre, east to west.

Several cellar walls in No 6 retained evidence of early fabric, probably of later 17th century date – perhaps part of Sarah Browne's remodelling of the Castle inn in 1651. These were built with roughly-faced chalk blocks and a small quantity of red brick, of a fabric and size dateable to anywhere between the mid 15th century and c. 1700. The sparing use of brick suggests these walls were built when bricks were still a relatively high status material, although the proximity of Hampton Court, a consumer of a large quantity of bricks, would have ensured their local availability as early as the 16th century. The front wall of No 6 had also been rebuilt during the later 17th century.

The lower level of the east-west wall dividing the front room of the cellar of No 7 was built with chalk on its northern side and brick on its southern face, and is likely to be of a similar date. Its alignment corresponded to a wall on the ground floor, which had divided the entrance hall/passage from the front room to its north. It is possible that the wall was only faced in brick on its southern side because it had faced onto a passage that provided access to a range of rooms set further back.

Most of the outer cellar walls in Nos 8–9 date to before c. 1700, although the one separating the front and back parts of No 8's cellar was probably built when an opening was made between the cellars of Nos 8 and 9 in the 19th century. An area of render scored with the inscription '1804' had been applied to 17th century brickwork in the front part of No 8's cellar. The main spine wall dividing Nos 8 and 9 as well as most of the internal walls in Nos 7 and 8 were datable to the 18th–19th century.

1912, the former boundaries had governed the nature of its growth and evolution. This was particularly evident in the cellars, and also in the orientation, at 90° to the street, of the hipped, tiled roof of the single-bay wide building behind the market frontage of No 6.

The complex 19th–20th century history of the site's ownership and use is well recorded in both maps and documents (*Fig. 109*). There were two large, 'double' properties – the rebuilt *Castle* inn (Nos 5–6) and a drapery business run by the Shrubsole family (Nos 8–9). By 1837, the *Castle* inn had ceased trading and the building was divided, No 6 continuing as the *Castle Tap* inn under the ownership of Henry Smith, and No 5 being converted into a shop under the ownership of Mr Fricker (*Fig. 108*).

From 1792, the single property between them (No 7) was a bank, also run by the Shrubsoles until 1894, and subsequently by Parr's. Like the surviving roof of the range at the rear of the former *Castle* inn at No 6 Market Place, the attic space at No 7, with its queen post truss system, also survived until demolition in 1999. The tithe map of 1841 shows ancillary buildings further back in the property.

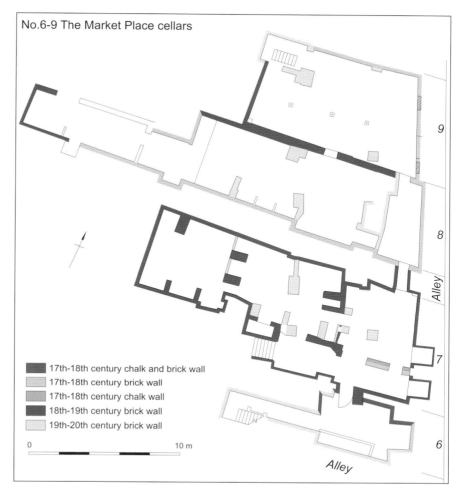

No.6-9 The Market Place cellars

- ■ 17th-18th century chalk and brick wall
- □ 17th-18th century brick wall
- ▨ 17th-18th century chalk wall
- ■ 18th-19th century brick wall
- □ 19th-20th century brick wall

0   10 m

Figure 107: Plan of 17th century and earlier cellar remains beneath the Market Place frontage at Charter Quay.

Figure 108: Reconstructed elevation of the buildings at Nos 5-9 Market Place in the late 19th century.

By 1870, Nos 8–9 had been extensively refurbished, this property, by then, also being owned by Parr. Its façade had been remodelled by Decimus Burton (the architect responsible for the triumphal arch at Hyde Park Corner), an 1897 photograph showing the projecting fascia and balcony. Three years later, in 1873, the property was bought by Joseph Hide, who by then owned No 6 (*Fig. 110*), and after 1900 No 5 as well. In 1907, the reunified Nos 5–6 were refaced, the first floor comprising large plate glass windows, and the second floor retaining much of the 18th century detailing and roof construction.

There were also frequent alterations at Hide's property at Nos 8–9, records documenting numerous shop extensions, new workshops and stables in 1882, 1896, 1897, 1900, 1905, 1906 and 1910. The last of these turned the rear of the property into a small, single storey open plan shop, Hide's Department Store, the shop being lit by sky lights decorated with plaster panels that survived until demolition in 1999. Department stores, a French invention, were first introduced to Britain in London during the 1860s and 1870s. They used new building techniques to create large multi-storey palaces providing

Figure 109: Sequence of occupiers at Nos 5–9 Market Place in the 19th and 20th centuries.

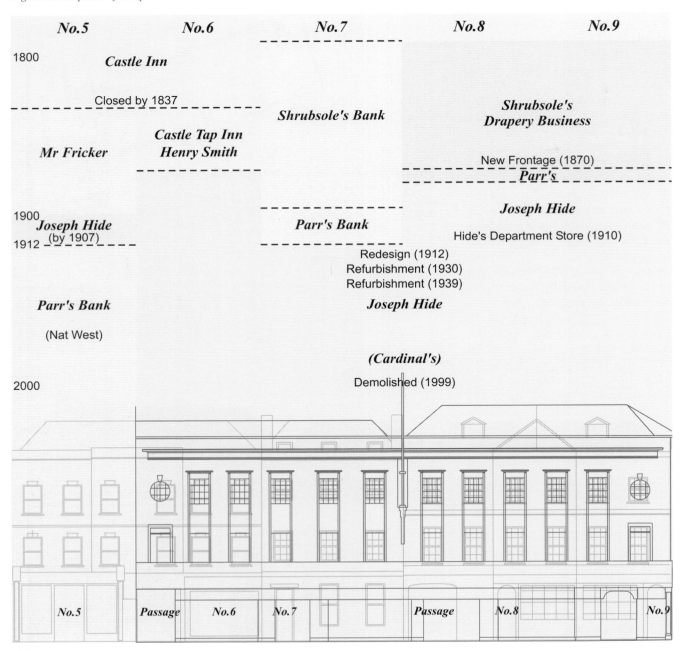

Figure 110: Nos 5 and 6 Market Place.

shopping facilities with an air of luxury and leisure catering for the middle class. One could buy in a single shop most items needed to furnish a home, from furniture and china, to carpets and ironmongery – as indicated on the 1910 proposal drawings.

The 1910 works also blocked the street end of the alley between Nos 7 and 8, which had previously allowed side access to both buildings as well as to the yards behind, although the alley survived as an external area to the rear. At No 7, Parr's Bank, a building with a three-bay frontage and three dormers set in a mansard roof with opposing chimneystacks, was now surrounded on three sides by properties owned by Joseph Hide, so in 1912 Parr and Hide swapped premises – Parr moving into No 5, and Hide into No 6. Parr had plans for a new bank at No 5 prepared by Walter Hewitt and Francis Garlich and demolished the existing building.

Hide was now able to get Edward Carter to redesign an enlarged store spanning Nos 6 to 9 Market Place. This involved extending the rear of Nos 6–7 in a similar open plan to Nos 8–9, but this time over two storeys.

The roof of No 7

Examination of the roof at No 7 indicated that the surviving queen post trusses (trusses with paired vertical posts set on the tie-beam and supporting plates or purlins) had been built on a substantial timber frame that was no longer present beneath third floor level. The attic had been partitioned in the past to form two rooms reached by a corridor at the rear of the building, and there was timber panelling and remnants of 19th century gas light fittings, as well as evidence of a fireplace at the south end. An internal lead lined gutter carried water from behind the front facade parapet to the rear of the property.

Behind the front roof there survived an oval roof lantern, a staircase and another room probably of late 19th to early 20th century origin. These features superseded an earlier lower pitch roof that was still visible behind the wall finish. The complicated nature of internal gullies and roof forms reflected the various phases of expansion and remodelling of earlier structures.

The entire attic floor had been linked, via the rooms and stairs in No 7, to a series of rooms, a single bay in depth, at the rear of Nos 8–9. These retained Victorian wallpapers, simple panelling and built in cupboards that were domestic in character, despite records showing the rooms' more recent use for storage. The rear walls in No 9 contained doors and a window that had been blocked when several rooms and a staircase were removed and a new slate-covered mansard roof was built. The proposal plans of 1930 indicate that these features were to be retained, signifying a fairly recent demolition date.

The ground floor walls were replaced by an irregular arrangement of iron columns to create more space (their positions reflecting the former property boundaries). Hide took with him from No 5 the *Castle* inn's 17th

57

century staircase, erecting it as the principal staircase in No 6, and so saving it from demolition. A stained glass window, depicting a castle and accompanied by a narrative informing that the Castle Inn had formerly stood on the site, was installed beside the stairs at first floor level (*Fig. 111*).

The department store was refurbished again in 1930 by Carter Young. Contemporary drawings provide valuable detail about the extent of the surviving historic fabric, showing that the second and attic floors were kept as residential apartments, with the ground and first floors being used for the shop. Despite the properties now being in single ownership, their haphazard development was still evident in the lack of a uniform façade, but this was to change in 1939 when the entire façade was remodelled by Leslie Norton (*Fig. 112*). The symmetry of the new design, incorporating circular windows and a decorative band between the first and second floor windows, was achieved by a thickening and levelling of different build lines.

However, there still remained a noticeable kink in the centre (where there was a tall flagpole), reflecting the division between Nos 6–7 and Nos 8–9. At the same time the rooms to the rear of Nos 8–9 were demolished and minor alterations and modifications made internally.

The rear of the plots were expanded again in 1966 to accommodate the further expansion of the department store, as well as changes of use in specific areas of the building. Lifts were added in 1974 and in 1984, and a new hairdressing salon created within the 17th century range at the south of the building. Unfortunately, this resulted in the loss of some of the building's fittings, including a staircase and an internal wall associated with this range. The store continued under Hide's name until 1977, when it was brought by the House of Fraser and became Cardinal's. This was closed in 1986 bringing to an end the oldest retail business in Kingston, and one of the oldest in Britain.

The Cardinal's department store building demolished in 1999 at Nos 6–9 Market Place displayed few external clues as to its long and complex history. Yet even its modern façade, the latest of a series of recent alterations, if examined closely, hinted at the presence and positions of former buildings on the site. Behind that façade, however, in the layout of its cellars, in the arrangement of its foundations and other features revealed by excavations, and in the structure of its roof, was to be found clear evidence of the original boundaries of some of Kingston's earliest properties, set out in the medieval burgage plot some 900 years before.

Figure 111:
Mid–17th century staircase from the Castle inn relocated from No 5 to No 6 in 1912.

Figure 112: Cardinal's department store on the Market Place frontage at Charter Quay prior to demolition.

58

Conclusions

The redevelopment of Charter Quay has provided a unique opportunity to excavate a large area in the historic centre of Kingston upon Thames between the town's ancient market place and the River Thames, the two features most vital to its commercial and economic life. Kingston, a royal estate centre at which a number of Saxon kings were crowned, was the location, from around 1170, of the first bridge across the Thames upriver of London, so helping the town develop through the medieval and later periods as a thriving inland port and market centre. The excavations amply fulfilled their potential to uncover, on the one hand, the processes of urban development and change, and on the other, specific details of the lives of the town's residents, business people, workers and visitors.

The excavations, combined with historical research, have revealed the steady evolution of the urban townscape, uncovering evidence of the formal apportionment of land into burgage plots along the central market place, the cycle of building, demolition, rebuilding and extension in response to the demands of economic and demographic growth, the expansion of settlement and riverside industry beyond the early limits of the town, and the continual reclamation of land flanking the River Thames and the Hogsmill. And it has shown how the earliest of planning decisions taken by the town authorities had a lasting impact on the layout and appearance of that townscape into the modern era.

However, the excavations have also provided the details necessary to populate that townscape with the people that ran its businesses, worked in its industries, cooked and ate in its inns and constructed its buildings. We can glimpse, for instance, the hand of the 12th century carpenter who cut the complex scarf joint used in the wall-plate of a market place building, the hand perhaps of the fishmonger, slightly tilting his bucket in the Hogsmill channel so that moving water would keep its contents fresh, the hand of the cook at the *Saracen's Head* preparing a lavish meal for her guests, themselves perhaps courtiers or diplomats staying in the town to be near the royal palace at Hampton Court, or the hand of Sarah Browne, proprietor of the *Castle Inn*, running her fingers over her initials she had had inscribed on inn's new brickwork and carved into its newly installed staircase. We can see the hands also of the boat builders, bakers, shoe makers, maltsters and butchers, all of them representing a diversity and continuity of town life over some 900 years.

The range and variety of finds from Charter Quay are what one would expect from a large urban archaeological excavation, but some have provided important new information, adding significantly to our knowledge of aspects of medieval and post-medieval life. However, all the findings together have combined to create a more complete and more comprehensible picture of the history of Kingston and its inhabitants from the founding of the town to the present day.

Acknowledgements

Wessex Archaeology would like to acknowledge the assistance and facilities provided by St George who commissioned the work, and in particular Deborah Aplin (Project Director), Ken Davies, Joe Bracchi, Steve Brook and Andy Healey for their role in ensuring the smooth running and successful completion of the fieldwork. In this respect we would also like to thank the staff of the groundworks contractors, O'Rourkes and Coinfords, for their co-operation and assistance during various stages of the excavation and watching brief.

The desk-based assessment and subsequent specification for evaluation and excavation was prepared by Duncan Hawkins of CgMs Consulting Ltd, archaeological consultants for the project. Duncan Hawkins was instrumental in co-ordinating the programme of archaeological work as well as monitoring progress, and we would also like to thank him for providing us with the benefit of his local knowledge of Kingston. The collaborative role of English Heritage and particularly Ken Whittaker, formerley Archaeology Advisor, Greater London Archaeology Advisory Service (GLAAS), is also acknowledged.

Thanks are extended to Martin Higgins, formerly Buildings Conservation Officer of the Royal Borough of Kingston upon Thames, for his advice in various respects. The staff at Kingston police station and Woolworth's store kindly allowed access to the roofs of their buildings on several occasions for photographic purposes.

The project was managed for Wessex Archaeology by Jonathan Nowell, with the fieldwork directed by Phil Andrews assisted by Bob Davis and Hilary Valler. The excavation team comprised Sue Fielding, Tessa Gent, Barry Hennessy, Phil Jefferson, Jim Chapman, Alan Dixon, Cornelius Barton, Jane Liddle, Matt Wright and Jenni Morrison. Finds co-ordination, data entry and the production of post-excavation plans was undertaken by Hilary Valler, and the timbers recorded by Bob Davis with assistance from Nick Molteno, Sue Fielding, Phil Jefferson and Gemma Smith.

Documentary research, which formed an integral part of the entire project, was undertaken by Dr Christopher Phillpotts. Finds analysis was co-ordinated by Lorraine Mepham (Finds Manager) who has also reported on several categories of finds (pottery, metalwork, leather and worked bone). Other finds reports have been prepared by Hilary Valler (ceramic building material, worked stone, glass and clay pipes) and Nicholas Wells (coins). The environmental analysis was co-ordinated by Michael J. Allen (Environmental Manager), with initial processing undertaken by Hayley Clark and Sarah Wyles. The assessment of the animal bone was carried out by Pippa Smith, and species identifications of the timbers were provided by Rowena Gale. Subsequent environmental analysis and reporting was carried out by Sheila Hamilton-Dyer (animal bone), Pat Hinton (plant remains), Alan Clapham (waterlogged plant remains), Rowena Gale (charcoal) and Enid Allison (insects). Other specialist reports have been provided by Ian Tyers (dendrochronology), Bill McCann (TRM dating), Andrew Harris and Jon Lowe (building recording), and Ken Sabel (brick structures).

Nathalie Cohen and Robin Neilsen at the Museum of London Archaeological Services (MoLAS) are thanked for making available the archive and discussing various aspects of the 1988-90 archaeological investigations at Charter Quay which have been incorporated in this report. We are particularly grateful to the staff at Kingston History Centre for providing copies of several photographs, prints and maps from their extensive collection which have been reproduced here. Roy Stephenson and Andy Chopping of the Museum of London Specialist Services (MoLSS) kindly arranged provision of the Kingston-ware photographs.

The archaeological excavation stimulated considerable local interest, and we are grateful to June Sampson who provided much information on Kingston and has taken a particular interest in the Charter Quay site. The seminal essays of Joan Wakeford and the recently published history of Kingston by Shaan Butters have also provided essential information on the development of the town.

This publication represents a synthesis of the reports prepared by the various specialists, built around the structural sequence (prepared by Phil Andrews) and the documentary work (undertaken by Christopher Phillpotts), set within the wider archaeological and historical framework of Kingston (provided by Duncan Hawkins). The draft report was read and commented on by Jonathan Nowell, and Andrew Powell undertook the final editing to produce a co-ordinated manuscript. The illustrations and photographs are by Karen Nichols, Linda Coleman, Liz James and Elaine Wakefield. The text was prepared for publication by Julie Gardiner. Karen Nichols has been responsible for the overall design and typesetting of this illustrated history of the Charter Quay site.

Endnotes

1. Nielsen 1989a, 1989b, 1989c, 1991
2. Hawkins 1996a
3. Whittaker 1997
4. Penn and Rolls 1981; Hawkins 1997b
5. Hawkins 1998, 271
6. Hawkins 1996b
7. Hawkins 1998, 273
8. Potter 1988, 140
9. Pearce/Vince 1988; Miller/Stephenson 1999
10. Vince and Jenner 1991
11. Pearce and Vince 1988
12. Pearce et al 1985
13. Tyers 2000
14. Hill and Woodger 1999, 30-35
15. Brown 1986, 42
16. Goodburn 1995
17. Potter 1988, 144-5
18. Wilson 1973
19. Crossley and Aberg 1986
20. Charleston 1984
21. Galloway et al 1996
22. Hinton and Nelson 1980
23. Woodforde 1983, 44
24. Cox 1996

Bibliography

Brown, R.J., 1986. *Timber-Framed Buildings of England*. London: Robert Hale

Charleston, R.J., 1984, The glass. In J.P. Allen, *Medieval Finds from Exeter, 1971–1980*. Exeter Archaeological Report 3, 258–78

Crossley, D.W. and Aberg, F.A. 1986. Sixteenth century glass-making in Yorkshire at furnaces at Hutton and Rosedale, North Riding 1968–1971. *Post-Medieval Archaeology* 6, 107–59

Cox, M. 1996. *Life and Death in Spitalfields 1700–1850*. York: Council for British Archaeology

Galloway, J.A., Keene, D. and Murphy, M. Fuelling the city: the production of firewood and distributon of fuel in London's region, 1290–1400. *Economic History Review* 69 (3), 447–72

Goodburn, D. 1995. Beyond the post-hole: notes on stratigraphy and timber buildings from a London perspective. In E. Shepherd (ed.), *Interpreting Stratigraphy* 5, 43–52

Hawkins, D. 1996a. *Archaeological Desk-Based Assessment of the Charter Quay Site, Kingston upon Thames*. Unpublished client report (Lawson Price Environmental)

Hawkins, D. 1996b. Roman Kingston upon Thames: A landscape of rural settle-ments. *London Archaeologist* 8(2), 46–50

Hawkins, D. 1998. Anglo-Saxon Kingston: a shifting pattern of settlement. *London Archaeologist* 8(10), 271–8

Hawkins, D. 2003. From Norman estate centre to Angevin town: Kingston upon Thames urban origins. *London Archaeologist* 10(4), 95–101

Hill, J. and Woodger, A. 1999, *Excavations at 72–75 Cheapside/ 83–95 Queen Street, City of London*. London: Museum of London Archaeology Service, 30–5

Hinton, M. and Nelson, S. 1980. Medieval and later pottery made in Kingston upon Thames. *London Archaeologist* 3(14), 377–83

Miller, P. and Stephenson, R. 1999. *A 14th-century Pottery Site in Kingston upon Thames, Surrey*, London: Museum of London Archaeology Service Study Series 1

Nielsen, R. 1989a. *Results and Implications of Preliminary Archaeological Site Evaluations on South Side of Hogsmill Creek*. Unpublished DGLA Developer Report (Museum of London)

Nielsen, R. 1989b. *Results and Implications of Preliminary Archaeological Site Evaluation on Site 4 (Emms Boatyard)*. Unpublished DGLA Developer Report (Museum of London)

Nielsen, R. 1989c. *Results and Implications of Preliminary Archaeological Site Evaluations on North Side of Hogsmill Creek (Sites 1 and 3)*. Unpublished DGLA Developer Report (Museum of London)

Nielsen, R. 1991. *Report of Archaeological Excavations on Site 5 (Odeon Cinema)*. Unpublished DGLA Developer Report (Museum of London)

Pearce, J. and Vince, A. 1988. *A Dated Type Series of London Medieval Pottery, part 4: Surrey Whitewares*. London & Middlesex Archaeological Society Paper 10

Pearce, J.E., Vince, A. and Jenner, M.A. 1985. *A Dated Type-Series of London Medieval Pottery part 2: London-type ware*. London & Middlesex Archaeological Society Special Paper

Penn, J.S. and Rolls, J.D. 1981. Problems in the quaternary development of the Thames Valley around Kingston. 'A framework for Archaeology'. *Transactions of the London & Middlesex Archaeological Society* 32, 1–11

Potter, G. 1988. The medieval bridge and waterfront at Kingston upon Thames. In G.L. Good, R.H. Jones and M.W. Ponsford (eds), *Waterfront Archaeology*, 140–54. London: Council for British Archaeology Research Report. 74

Tyers, I. 2000. *Tree-ring spot dates from Charter Quay, Kingston, Greater London*. ARCUS Dendrochronology, Project report 551

Vince, A. and Jenner, A. 1991. The Saxon and early medieval pottery of London. In A. Vince (ed.), *Aspects of Saxon and Norman London 2: finds and environmental evidence*, 19–119. London & Middlesex Archaeological Society Special Paper 12.

Whittaker, K. 1997. *Medieval and Post-medieval Urbanism: the market town of Kingston upon Thames research project outline*. London: English Heritage

Wilson, C.A. 1973. *Food and Drink in Britain*. London: Constable

Woodforde, J. 1983. *The Strange Story of False Teeth*. London: Routledge & Kegan Paul

Internet Reports

Index of Specialist Reports

Dating

Tree-ring spot-dates, by Ian Tyers

The Archaeomagnetic dating of two 14th-15th century hearths, by W.A. McCann, The Clark Laboratory, Museum of London Archaeology Service

The brickwork at Nos 6-9 Market Place, by Ken Sabel

Environmental

Animal bones, by Sheila Hamilton-Dyer

Charcoal from 15th /16th -17th century deposits, by Rowena Gale

Insects from a late 13th/early 14th century hearth, by E.P. Allison

Plant remains, by Pat Hinton

Waterlogged plant remains, by Alan Clapham

Finds

Ceramic building material and fired clay, by Hilary Valler

Clay pipes, by Hilary Valler

Coins, by Nicholas A. Wells

Glass, by Hilary Valler and Lorraine Mepham

Leather, by Lorraine Mepham

Metal objects, by Lorraine Mepham

Pottery, by Lorraine Mepham

Worked bone, by Lorraine Mepham

Worked stone, by Hilary Valler

http://www.wessexarch.co.uk/projects/london/charter_quay